Kindle Touch™
FOR
DUMMIES®
PORTABLE EDITION

by Leslie H. Nicoll and Harvey Chute

D0967361

WILEY

John Wiley & Sons, Inc.

Kindle Touch™ For Dummies® Portable Edition

Published by
John Wiley & Sons, Inc.
111 River Street
Hoboken, NJ 07030-5774

www.wiley.com

Copyright © 2012 by John Wiley & Sons, Inc., Hoboken, New Jersey

Published by John Wiley & Sons, Inc., Hoboken, New Jersey

Published simultaneously in Canada

WILEY

About the Authors

Leslie H. Nicoll, Ph.D., is a wife, mother, and nurse, as well as a lifelong voracious reader. She purchased her first Kindle in April 2008 at the urging of her daughter Hannah. The plan was that they would share the device but within a week, Leslie realized the futility of that idea and was quickly placing an order for a second Kindle.

Leslie has never been one to do things halfway and she quickly threw herself into learning everything she could about the Kindle — and helping others do the same. For many months she informally maintained "The Amazon Kindle FAQ" at the Amazon Kindle forum. In September 2008 she pulled the questions and answers together and published it as a Kindle book. In November 2008 it became the number one selling "how-to" guide on Amazon.

Leslie has owned every version of the Kindle that has been released. She also happily reads Kindle books on her iPhone and laptop, using the free Kindle app for those devices. Still, she admits a preference for the clear and crisp eInk screen on her latest generation graphite Kindle Touch with Wi-Fi and 3G.

This is the second *For Dummies* book that Leslie has co-authored; in addition, she has written extensively in the professional nursing literature with a resume that boasts books, book chapters, and more than 120 peer-reviewed articles.

Harvey Chute is the owner and Webmaster of the independent Kindle discussion forum, KindleBoards (www.kindleboards.com). The site is an active hub for Kindle owners, with 50,000 registered members and over one million posts about all things Kindle.

As a lover of reading, innovative technology, and gadgets, Harvey has had a natural passion for Amazon's Kindle since the first generation of the device was released in 2007.

Harvey is a program manager for a systems integration company. He is the author or technical editor for six other *For Dummies* books. His interests include software development, gadgets, music, photography, and enjoying life with his wife and three daughters.

Dedication

Leslie dedicates this e-book to her husband Tony, who happily supports her Kindle addiction, even though he prefers to listen to books on his iPhone!

Harvey dedicates this e-book to his wife, Carrie, who is affectionately known as *KindleWidow* in the KindleBoards online forums.

Authors' Acknowledgments

Leslie wants to thank the community of people she has met through online Kindle forums, in particular KindleBoards. To be able to interact with a community of thousands of folks who share her love of reading is truly a wonderful experience. She also wants to thank Tony, her husband, and Lance and Hannah, her children, for their ongoing love and support.

Harvey wants to acknowledge the members of KindleBoards for the insight, good humor, and helpfulness demonstrated by them in thousands of discussion threads. And he appreciates their great indie e-book recommendations! He especially thanks the board's moderators — Ann, Betsy, Heather, Leslie, Lynn, and Geoffrey — who do so much to make the boards a useful and enjoyable destination for Kindle owners.

Publisher's Acknowledgments

We're proud of this book; please send us your comments at `http://dummies.custhelp.com`. For other comments, please contact our Customer Care Department within the U.S. at 877-762-2974, outside the U.S. at 317-572-3993, or fax 317-572-4002.

Some of the people who helped bring this book to market include the following:

Acquisitions and Editorial

Project Editor: Blair J. Pottenger

Senior Acquisitions Editor: Katie Mohr

Copy Editor: Jen Riggs

Technical Editor: Betsy True

Editorial Manager: Kevin Kirschner

Editorial Assistant: Amanda Graham

Sr. Editorial Assistant: Cherie Case

Cover Photo: ©iStockphoto.com / Anthia Cumming (background); image of device by Holly Wittenberg

Cartoons: Rich Tennant (`www.the5thwave.com`)

Composition Services

Senior Project Coordinator: Kristie Rees

Layout and Graphics: Christin Swinford

Proofreaders: Melissa Cossell, Susan Hobbs, Dwight Ramsey

Indexer: BIM Indexing & Proofreading Services

Publishing and Editorial for Technology Dummies

Richard Swadley, Vice President and Executive Group Publisher

Andy Cummings, Vice President and Publisher

Mary Bednarek, Executive Acquisitions Director

Mary C. Corder, Editorial Director

Publishing for Consumer Dummies

Kathleen Nebenhaus, Vice President and Executive Publisher

Composition Services

Debbie Stailey, Director of Composition Services

Contents at a Glance

Table of Contents

Introduction

For many, the Kindle family of e-readers has "rekindled" their love of reading. Whether it's the convenience of having an entire library stored on a 7.8-ounce device or the ability to enlarge the font so you can read more comfortably, Kindle users seem to be unanimous in their praise for this handy gadget. Even people uncertain about the idea of an e-reader tend to get hooked after they lay their eyes on the crisp, clear e-ink display — one that truly mimics a printed reading experience.

If you're new to the Kindle world, welcome to the club. If you're a seasoned pro who's owned every generation of the device since it first came out, we're pleased to count you among the readership. And if you fall somewhere in between, well, we're glad you're here, too. Our motto might be, "Kindle enthusiasts, unite!" We're here because of our love of reading, and we've discovered that Kindle e-readers, in particular, the Kindle Touch, make reading *better*. How? That's what we share with you in this book.

About This Book

This book is clear, practical, down-to-earth and full of helpful hints. It includes eight chapters, but you don't need to read them in order — each chapter stands on its own. So if you're interested in a particular topic, jump ahead to that chapter.

Chapter 1: Getting to Know Your Kindle Touch

This chapter includes a basic overview of the Kindle Touch, including how to navigate the touchscreen and a few shortcuts. We also discuss setting up your Kindle Touch, registering it at Amazon, getting Wi-Fi to work, and getting to know the basics about the e-ink display.

Chapter 2: Reading on Your Kindle Touch

Chapter 2 covers basic reading functions, including tips for finding content loaded on your Kindle Touch and effective use of collections to organize your reading material. This chapter also describes newer Kindle Touch features, such as lending e-books, borrowing e-books from the library and Amazon, and making updates on Facebook and Twitter from your Kindle Touch.

Chapter 3: Finding Content for Your Kindle Touch

You love to read and you're eager to get started — this is the chapter to turn to! We describe finding e-books at Amazon and other sources, including free e-books. We also detail how to search effectively at Amazon so that you can find hidden treasures.

Chapter 4: Putting Your Own Documents on Your Kindle Touch

Your Kindle Touch is useful not only for reading published e-books; you can also load your Kindle Touch with your personal documents. Carry around your documents on your Kindle Touch by transferring them from your computer. The chapter also covers how to convert a wide variety of documents into a Kindle-compatible format and what it means to store them in your archive at Amazon.

Chapter 5: Accessories: Making Your Kindle Touch Look Sharp

We discuss covers, skins, lights, and other add-ons in Chapter 5. Are accessories essential or just a fun way to dress up your Kindle Touch? You can decide after reading this chapter.

Chapter 6: Beyond Reading: Other Kindle Touch Features

This chapter takes you beyond the Kindle Touch reading experience, and into the Kindle Touch's capabilities as a web browser, music player, and audiobook reader.

Chapter 7: Troubleshooting

Having problems? Head here first! This chapter lays out the most common ailments that your Kindle Touch might encounter — and gives troubleshooting tips to resolve them quickly.

Chapter 8: Ten Helpful Kindle Touch Tips

This book concludes with ten tips, tricks, hints, shortcuts, and questions about the Kindle Touch.

Conventions Used in This Book

This book uses certain conventions to make it easy for readers to understand the techniques that are presented, whether they're shortcuts or keywords for searching the Kindle Store:

- ✔ **Bold:** Indicates an action you take on the touchscreen. The bold, numbered text in a numbered list indicates the action(s) you take to accomplish a task. Similarly, if you need to type something using the on-screen keyboard, those instructions will be printed in bold.

- ✔ *Italics:* Indicates a term we define. We also use italics to indicate a term you search for on the web. Italics are also used to indicate placeholder text. For example, in Chapter 4 we use italics on "yourname" in *yourname@* free.kindle.com and *yourname*@kindle.com.

✔ Monofont: Indicates a *URL* (a web address). Note that URLs are links; just tap the URL with your finger to go to that web page.

In addition to URLs, chapter and section references are links; just tap the chapter title or section listing to select it and then instantly jump to the place you chose.

Foolish Assumptions

This book is written about the latest generation e-ink Kindle, known as the Kindle Touch, which came out in November 2011. We assume that's the Kindle version you own, or at least have access to, to try out the tips, tricks, and procedures that we discuss.

We assume that you have some sort of computer (Windows or Mac) that has a USB port so that you can connect your Kindle Touch to the port with the USB cable that ships with the device.

We don't expect you to be a computer genius. However, we assume you know the basics of navigating on your computer, how to search the web, the difference between files and folders, and how to copy and paste items from one place to another. On the Internet, we assume you're familiar with Amazon and have an active account there to which you can log in.

Icons Used in This Book

For Dummies titles use icons to highlight a paragraph that contains a tip, warning, technical stuff, or something you want to remember. Look for the following icons in this book:

Quick hints, helpful tips, and other tidbits of information are included in the paragraphs that are highlighted with the bull's eye and arrow.

Tie a string on your finger and keep these things in mind. Remember items are mostly gleaned from our experience.

Although it's pretty hard to break a Kindle Touch, you can do things inadvertently that you might not be able to undo, such as permanently delete a favorite e-book. These pitfalls are highlighted with the little bomb in the Warning icon.

Occasionally, we provide details of interest to the technically curious. This nitty-gritty information is flagged with the Technical Stuff icon.

Where to Go from Here

Have fun exploring your Kindle Touch. For most activities, it's an intuitive and user-friendly device. This book helps you get started and guides you into some of the more advanced features that the Kindle Touch offers. Tap the screen on your Kindle Touch to advance to the next page and keep reading, or use the helpful links in the text and in the Table of Contents to jump to the section or chapter that covers a particular topic you're interested in.

If you want to go deeper with your Kindle Touch experience, consider joining an online Kindle forum. There you can share tips, e-book recommendations, and more with thousands of other Kindle owners.

With your Kindle Touch, it's a new world of reading where you have vast libraries of e-books at your fingertips. Enjoy the ride!

Chapter 1

Getting to Know Your Kindle Touch

*W*elcome to the wonderful world of Kindle reading. Getting started with your Kindle Touch is quick and easy, as you discover in this chapter. This chapter introduces the basic features of the Kindle Touch and discusses the first steps in becoming a successful *Kindler* (a Kindle user and reader). We cover some important tips to make your Kindle Touch come alive and help you understand the firmware that runs it.

Picking the Right Kindle Touch for You

The Kindle Touch has several options available to you — when you purchase your device, you need to decide which ones you want. Your choices include

> ✔ **How you connect to the Internet:** Your choices are a Wi-Fi only model (the Kindle Touch), or a 3G + Wi-Fi model (the Kindle Touch 3G).

Amazon uses different names for its Kindle Touch models. Amazon calls the Wi-Fi only model the Kindle Touch and the 3G + Wi-Fi model the Kindle Touch 3G. Throughout this book, we use Kindle Touch when referring to both models (for example, when the way you do something on the device is the same regardless of which model you own). When we need to differentiate between the two models, we do so by calling them the Wi-Fi only Kindle Touch and the Kindle Touch 3G.

✔ **Whether you want offers and ads displayed on your screensaver:** You can purchase a Kindle Touch that has special offers and sponsored screensavers, or you can buy one with non-special offers (or traditional screensavers).

Mixing and matching among these choices gives you four versions of the Kindle Touch from which to choose. The cheapest ($99) is the Wi-Fi only Kindle Touch with special offers; the most expensive ($189) is the Kindle Touch 3G with traditional screensavers. How do you choose?

We start with deciding on the method you use to connect to the Internet.

Deciding between Wi-Fi only or 3G + Wi-Fi

How do you decide whether you want a Wi-Fi only Kindle Touch or the Kindle Touch 3G? Good question!

The Wi-Fi only Kindle Touch requires a Wi-Fi wireless Internet connection to download content from Amazon and other sources. You may already have this set up in your home and could use this as your Wi-Fi hotspot. You can also connect your Kindle Touch to Wi-Fi hotspots in public locations, such as Starbucks and McDonald's. On the other hand, Kindle Touch 3G operates on the same cellular network as cellphones and, in essence, is available to you everywhere — in your home, office, car, and public areas such as airports, train stations, and restaurants. While 3G is widely available, there are places in the U.S. that don't have coverage. Amazon provides a coverage map which can be accessed at www.amazon.com/gp/help/customer/display.html?nodeId=200375890&#whispintl.

Be aware that there is no additional charge for the 3G, such as a dataplan that is required for a cellphone. Amazon covers the 3G costs.

In addition to 3G cellular networks, the Kindle Touch 3G can also access and utilize Wi-Fi connections when they're available and in range.

If you anticipate needing to use the wireless only when you're at home or connected to another Wi-Fi network, the Wi-Fi only Kindle Touch is a good choice. (Remember that you need to know how your Wi-Fi network is set up to connect to it — including the password.) On the other hand, if you don't have access to Wi-Fi, travel regularly, or just love the magic of being able to download an e-book in less than a minute, anywhere, any time, you may prefer the Kindle Touch 3G.

Choosing between traditional screensavers or special offers and sponsored screensavers

In 2011, Amazon came out with a new option: special offers and sponsored screensavers — in other words, advertising on your Kindle Touch. In exchange for this, Amazon discounted the price by $40.

Reading online forums, user reaction to this change has been mixed, but mostly positive. Those who are opposed don't like having advertising on their Kindle Touch, period. On the other hand, many appreciate the discounts and special offers on Kindle e-books and accessories, as well as other products, such as clothing and electronics, that are sold through Amazon. The special offers appear as screensavers and as one small bar promoting the offer at the bottom of the Home screen. No advertising occurs inside the Kindle Touch content.

If you choose a Kindle Touch with special offers and decide you don't like them, you can unsubscribe for $40 — the difference in the price that you paid originally. Go to the Manage Your Kindle page for your Amazon account (www.amazon. com/myk), choose Manage Your Devices, and click Edit in the Special Offers column to unsubscribe. You may re-subscribe later if you wish, but you will not receive a refund.

The $40 will include sales tax for those states that include sales tax on Amazon purchases.

A brief history of the Kindle family of e-readers

The first Amazon Kindle became available in 2007, and sold out in less than six hours. Many users back-ordered their Kindles and waited months to receive them. The following year, when Oprah Winfrey announced on her television show that the Kindle was her "new favorite gadget," sales skyrocketed, and again, the Kindle went out of stock. For two years in a row, the Kindle wasn't available for Christmas purchases!

In 2009, Jeff Bezos, accompanied by author Stephen King at the press conference, announced the second generation Kindle. Also in 2009, the Kindle DX — the larger Kindle — and Kindle applications for the PC, Mac, and iPhone became available. To the joy of readers around the globe, an international version of the Kindle also came out in the fall of that year.

The third generation Kindle, known as the Kindle Keyboard, became available in 2010; it was the first Kindle offered with Wi-Fi only or 3G + Wi-Fi. A few months after it was released, Amazon started offering a version of the device with the special offers and sponsored screensavers.

The Kindle had a windfall year in 2011, with three new devices announced and released in the span of two months. The Kindle family now includes a basic Wi-Fi only model, priced at $79; the Kindle Touch, which is the focus of this book; and the Kindle Fire, an Android tablet that came out in November.

The Kindle Touch builds on the best of the past and adds a number of new innovations — most notably, the touchscreen. Like other Kindle readers, the screen uses *e-ink* — a technology that uses actual particles of ink sandwiched between two layers of polymer to create the images you see on the screen. E-ink also allows you to read in direct sunlight. The size of the display is 6 inches; overall the size is 11 percent smaller than the Kindle Keyboard. The device weighs 7.5 or 7.8 ounces (the 3G model is a tiny bit heavier). E-book storage is 4GB (with approximately 3GB available to the user), which allows a library of approximately 3,000 e-books and other content to be maintained on the device. With minimal use of wireless, the battery charge can last up to two months based upon a half-hour of daily reading time.

With the special offers, your screensavers change periodically. Some people, even if they don't take advantage of the discounts, like the variety of pictures that are shown. The *traditional* screensavers — that is, non-special offers — on the Kindle Touch have been updated from those shown on all the earlier Kindle versions. The new screensavers show a variety of pictures but no people. Everyone seems unanimous in their delight that the pictures of the deceased authors (Agatha Christie, John Steinbeck, and so on) are gone!

Price is a consideration when deciding among these options. The best bargain is the Wi-Fi only Kindle Touch with special offers at $99; Kindle Touch 3G with special offers is $149. Non-special offer models cost $139 (Wi-Fi only Kindle Touch) and $189 (Kindle Touch 3G). Note that even with the Kindle Touch 3G, you don't have to worry about any additional fees or commitments, which you might have with a cellphone data plan, because Amazon covers those costs.

Getting to Know Your Kindle Touch

Figure 1-1 illustrates the bottom of your Kindle Touch, which is where you find the power button, headphone jack, and USB port. There is only one other button on the Kindle Touch: the Home button, the four raised bars on the bottom-front edge (see Figure 1-1). The Home button is aptly named: Whenever you press it, it takes you back to the first page of your Home screen. If your swiping, tapping, and touching has gotten you hopelessly lost within your Kindle Touch, just press the Home button to go Home.

Power modes: Sleep, on, and off

To turn on the Kindle Touch, press the Power button and then release. The first time you use your Kindle Touch, it goes through a booting process that may take a few minutes to complete. After that's done, you see the Home screen, which lists a welcome letter, the Kindle User's Guide, and two built-in dictionaries: the *New Oxford American Dictionary*

(Oxford University Press) and the *Oxford Dictionary of English* (Oxford University Press) on a brand-new Kindle Touch. If you have purchased content while waiting for your Kindle Touch to arrive, those e-books appear on the Home screen when the wireless is turned on for the first time and the e-books are downloaded. (By the way, the Kindle Touch uses the *New Oxford American Dictionary* to look up words. You can change this to the *Oxford Dictionary of English,* or any other dictionary that you might buy and load onto your Kindle Touch, by tapping the Menu button and tapping Settings. The option to change the dictionary is the last item in the list.)

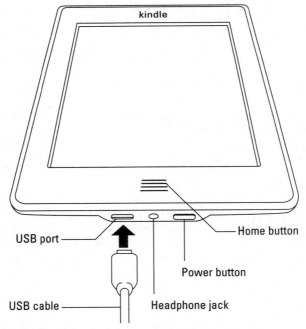

Figure 1-1: The bottom edge of the Kindle Touch.

Books will show up if the device is already registered to your account. If it's not already registered, you'll be prompted to register the device. For the Wi-Fi only Kindle Touch, the first thing that happens after the wireless is turned on is that you will have to connect to your router, so you will need the password.

When the Kindle Touch is plugged into a power source and is charging, the charge indicator light (located next to the power button) glows amber. When the device is fully charged, the light turns green.

 The Kindle Touch ships with only a USB cable for charging — it does not include a plug adapter. You can purchase a plug adapter separately from Amazon for $14.99. Other USB plug adapters, such as the one for the iPhone, are compatible with the Kindle Touch. In the absence of any of these, charge your Kindle Touch through a USB port connected to your computer.

The Kindle Touch has three modes, Sleep, on, and off:

✔ **To put the Kindle Touch in Sleep mode,** press the power button and release. When the Kindle Touch is in Sleep mode, a screensaver appears on the screen.

✔ **To turn on the Kindle Touch,** press the power button and release. You see the page that you last viewed before the device went into Sleep mode or was turned off.

✔ **To turn off the Kindle Touch,** press the power button and hold it until the charge indicator light blinks and the screen goes blank. This takes approximately 5 seconds.

✔ **To restart the Kindle Touch,** press and hold the power button for approximately 35 seconds, then release. The screen goes blank, after which the Kindle logo appears and the reboot sequence begins. You can also restart the Kindle Touch on the device by tapping the Menu button from the Home screen, tapping Settings, and then tapping Menu again. Restart is one of the menu options that appears in the list.

 In general, you don't need to turn off your Kindle Touch; just put it in Sleep mode. The device automatically goes into Sleep mode after ten minutes of inactivity. The Kindle Touch uses its battery power only for page turns, so there's no difference in battery usage between entering Sleep mode and turning off the Kindle Touch.

The only time you absolutely need to turn off your Kindle Touch is when you're on a plane during takeoff and landing, when passengers are asked that all portable electronic devices be turned off.

If you turn off your Kindle Touch (or don't put it in Sleep mode), make sure you're at the Home screen. Some users have reported problems with the Kindle Touch losing your place in the book if it's turned off with the book open. This isn't an issue with Sleep mode, however, which is another reason why Sleep mode is preferred over completely turning off your Kindle Touch on a routine basis.

Navigating with the touchscreen on your Kindle Touch

Prior versions of the Kindle e-reader had a variety of buttons on the device to navigate through e-books and other content. The Kindle Touch has a touchscreen — revolutionizing how you move around the screen and in books and other content. Even if you're a seasoned Kindle owner, you need to discover some new techniques for navigation. The following is a primer to get you started.

The basics: Tap, swipe, tap and hold, pinch, and stretch

The e-ink screen on your Kindle Touch is touch-sensitive, so it can detect your finger taps and movements. This gives you an easy and intuitive way to control your Kindle Touch.

All your common uses of the Kindle Touch — opening books, turning pages, placing bookmarks, and so on — involve a handful of simple touchscreen gestures, such as finger taps and swipes. For the most part, these gestures are used consistently throughout your use of Kindle Touch. (We point out the few cases where the behavior is a bit different than you might expect.)

We begin by examining how and when you use different finger motions as well as where on the screen you use them.

Tapping

A simple *tap* is the most common gesture you use with Kindle Touch. When an onscreen button appears, for example, you tap the button to activate it. When you view a list of your e-books, tapping an e-book opens it. And when you're reading an e-book, you tap to *page forward* (display the next page), *page backward* (display the previous page), or bring up a menu of commands. The effect of tapping a book's page depends on which part of the screen you tap; we discuss the three *tap zones* of a displayed page in the "Regions of the touchscreen" section later in this chapter.

Swiping right or left

Sliding your finger (or *swiping*) from right to left horizontally on the screen causes you to page forward. When reading a book, this is an alternative to tapping to advance the page. The motion is akin to flipping a paper page in a printed book.

Paging backward, of course, is accomplished with the reverse motion: a left-to-right horizontal swipe.

When viewing a list of books on the Home screen, a swipe motion — instead of a tap — is needed to page forward and backward. A tap on the title of a book (or other content) on the Home screen opens the item for reading.

A little experimentation with swiping shows that you need only to slide your finger a short distance. Most people don't need to change their hand position from how they naturally hold the Kindle Touch in order to swipe — or tap — to move around the pages in a book.

Swiping up or down

From within a book, swiping up on a page advances the book to its next chapter. Swiping downward, naturally, positions you back to the previous chapter. If book doesn't have chapter breaks set by its publisher, a swipe up or down has no effect.

Tapping and holding

Tapping and holding (sometimes dubbed a *long tap*) occurs when you touch the screen and hold your finger to it for a couple of seconds before releasing. In general, this causes a special action to happen, depending on what you're viewing at the time.

For example, when viewing a page of an e-book, you can tap and hold a word to bring up its dictionary definition. When viewing a list of e-books, a long tap on a particular e-book brings up a list of options for that e-book, including adding it to a collection, reading its description, or moving it to your archive of Kindle books at Amazon. If you tap and hold the title of an e-book sample that's listed on your Home screen, you can delete it from the device. If you acquired the e-book from a source other than Amazon, you can't move it to the archive of Kindle books at Amazon — your choice is to delete it.

Depending on where you obtained a book or other content, you'll have different options for deleting or moving. The Remove from Device option means the e-book is available in your archive of Kindle books at Amazon; that is, you either purchased the e-book from Amazon or it's an archived personal document that you e-mailed to your Kindle Touch. The Delete option displays with samples that you've downloaded from Amazon and unarchived content acquired from another source.

Deleting an e-book — that is, deleting an e-book not archived with your Kindle content at Amazon — is permanent. Make sure you have a backup on your computer if you don't want to get rid of the e-book forever.

When using the onscreen keyboard, you can access variations of certain letters with a tap and hold on that letter. For example, a tap and hold on the letter "e" brings up a row of letters on the keyboard with accent marks and other diacriticals.

Pinching and stretching

When reading an e-book, place two of your fingers on the touchscreen and slide them closer together. This *pinch* motion decreases the e-book's font size. Place two of your fingers on the screen and *stretch* them farther apart to increase the font size.

The text gets bigger or smaller, in real time, as you make the stretching or pinching motion, respectively — but there is somewhat of a lag. You may find that slowly moving your fingers helps. Also, you only have to move your fingers a small distance to have font size take effect on the screen.

Regions of the touchscreen

The screen of your Kindle Touch is set up with *EasyReach tap zones* — these are designed to let you turn pages effortlessly with one finger of either hand. Figure 1-2 illustrates the tap zones and their measurements. The following list explains each zone:

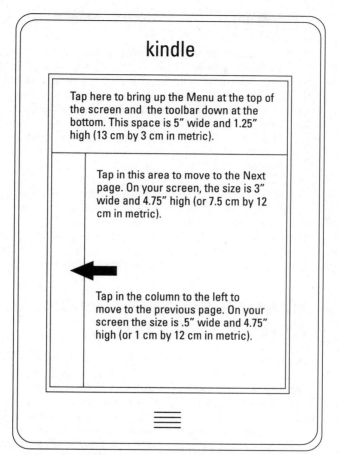

Figure 1-2: EasyReach tap zones on the Kindle Touch screen.

- ✔ The largest zone, the **central square,** is where you mainly tap. Within an e-book or e-magazine, a quick tap advances you to the next page. Within an e-book with chapter navigation enabled, a swipe from top to bottom in this zone moves you back a chapter; swiping from the bottom up moves you ahead a chapter.

- ✔ A tap on the **left column** zone takes you back one page. In our experience, the left column is the zone that takes a bit of getting used to. This zone is only half an inch wide, which means your tapping has to be precise. That said, after you can visualize it on the screen, it's easier to remember where to tap.

✔ The last zone is the **top area.** A tap here brings up two toolbars. The top toolbar contains the Back button, the Kindle Store button, the Search field, and the Menu button. The toolbar at the bottom of the screen is where you find the Text button (labeled Aa), the Go To button, and the Sync or X-Ray button. Which of the latter is displayed depends on whether X-Ray is enabled in the e-book. We discuss all these buttons in the "Virtual buttons" section later in this chapter.

Within an e-book, but not on the Home screen, if you tap in the upper-right corner, you set a bookmark on the page. Tapping there again deletes the bookmark. You can also set a bookmark by tapping to bring up the toolbar, then tapping the Menu button and then tapping Add Bookmark. One tap versus three. Which is better? We leave that for you to decide.

Understanding the screens your Kindle Touch displays

Depending on where you are and what you're looking at, your Kindle Touch may have one or more screens available for viewing. The primary screen is the Home screen. The number of screens in your Home screen is determined by the amount of content on your device. Each screen can display seven or eight items, so if you have 56 items on your Kindle Touch (e-books, magazines, personal documents, and so on), your Home screen would be seven or eight pages (or screens) long. You can see the length of your Home screen in the upper-right corner where it displays Page *x* of *x*.

The Home screen on the Kindle Touch with special offers and sponsored screensavers displays seven items — one slot for content is taken up by the small special offer banner at the bottom of the screen.

An e-book may have hundreds of screens. The actual number varies from e-book to e-book, depending on its length. Within an e-book, the number of screens varies depending on what size font you read with and how many lines display on the screen.

At the bottom of the screen are some indicators of where you are in the book. On the bottom-right, you see a percentage for how far along you are in the e-book. To find out the total length of the book, tap the top of the screen to bring up the top and bottom toolbars. At the very bottom of the screen, you see the total length of the book in locations and (if enabled for the book you're reading) pages. All Kindle books have locations as a measure of their length and are calculated as bits of information encoded in the file. Locations typically number in the thousands in an e-book compared to hundreds of pages for a traditional book.

Having the actual page number (and not just locations) is a feature that was implemented in early 2011. The page number corresponds to the page number in the printed book. If the book exists only in e-book format, it doesn't have page numbers at the bottom of the screen.

For e-books that display page numbers, you may be curious as to which version of the printed book matches those page numbers. You can find this out by going to the "Product Details" for the Kindle e-book on Amazon. The matching print edition displays as the Page Numbers Source ISBN. "Product Details" can be found between the Editorial Reviews and Customer Reviews on the page for the Kindle book at Amazon.

When you open an e-book, a small bar displays at the top of the screen, listing the book's title, the Wi-Fi or 3G indicator (if wireless is turned on), the battery charge meter, and the time. When you turn the page, this bar disappears. Bringing up the toolbars makes this information reappear. Note that the location numbers and percentage of progress through the book always displays at the bottom of the screen.

Charging

On the bottom of the Kindle Touch is the USB port for the charging cable (refer to Figure 1-1). This is a standard micro-USB. Notice that the charging cord has a micro-USB on one end and a standard USB on the other. Plug the micro-USB into the Kindle. The standard USB can be plugged into your computer or into the plug adapter, which is plugged into an electrical wall socket. As we note earlier, the Kindle Touch doesn't ship with a plug adapter. You must purchase this separately. The Kindle Touch is compatible with other chargers, such as the one used for the iPhone; it's also compatible with the plug adapter that came with earlier generation Kindles (Kindle 2 and Kindle Keyboard).

The initial charging of the Kindle Touch takes about 4 hours. After that, charging via USB and computer takes about 3 hours. Charging with the Kindle plugged into an electrical socket is usually shorter, about 1 to 2 hours.

The battery charge meter is in the upper-right corner of the Home screen. We recommend recharging the battery when it has about a quarter of a charge remaining. You don't need to "top off" the battery on a daily or weekly basis.

You can read and use your Kindle Touch while it charges. When the Kindle Touch is plugged into an electrical socket, the display doesn't change. However, when the Kindle Touch is plugged into the USB on the computer, you see the following message:

> If you want to read or shop on your Kindle while continuing to charge over USB, please keep the USB cable attached, but eject your Kindle from your computer.

If you want to read on your Kindle Touch while it's connected to your computer, eject the device via the operating system but leave it physically connected (or plugged in) to the USB port. To eject your Kindle Touch:

- **In Windows 7, Vista, and Windows XP:** Either left- or right-click the Safely Remove Hardware icon in the lower-right corner of the taskbar and choose Eject Amazon Kindle. The screen returns to whatever was open previously.

- **In Mac OS X:** Press ⌘-E. You can also drag the Kindle icon from the desktop to the trash can, or choose File⇨ Eject.

The headphone jack

On the bottom of your Kindle Touch, between the USB port
and the power button, is the headphone jack (refer to
Figure 1-1). Use this if you want to privately listen to an
audiobook or while having books read to you through the
Text-to-Speech feature. (The Kindle Touch also has speakers
on the back at the bottom of the device, so headphones aren't
required.)

The Kindle Touch doesn't have a volume button. To change
the volume, tap the top of the screen to bring up the top
toolbar, tap the Menu button, and then tap Turn On Text-to-
Speech. A touch-sensitive volume control displays; tap it to
adjust. If you're listening to an audiobook, the volume control
displays on the page that contains the audiobook information
which shows when you open the audiobook and it starts
playing.

Virtual buttons

The Kindle Touch has two physical buttons on the device: the
Power button and the Home button, which we've discussed
already. Buttons that were on earlier versions of the Kindle,
such as Back and Font, are incorporated as virtual onscreen
buttons that you tap or fields into which you can enter
information. The virtual buttons, which we discuss in the
following sections, are illustrated in Figure 1-3.

Back button

The Back button is the left-pointing arrow (←) and is the first
button on the top toolbar. The Back button is similar to the
Back button on a web browser: It lets you retrace your steps
on the Kindle Touch. In some instances, the Back button acts
like the Home button; for example, if you open an e-book from
the Home screen, read a few pages, and then press the Back
button, you return to the Home screen — not the previous
page you looked at.

Back button   Search field
          Kindle Store button   Menu button

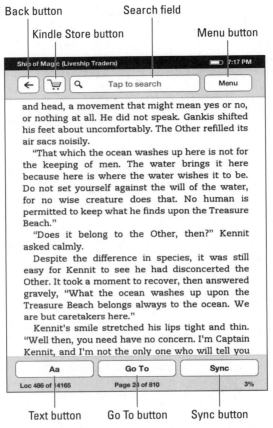

Text button   Go To button   Sync button

Figure 1-3: The top and bottom toolbars illustrating the virtual buttons of the Kindle Touch.

In an e-newspaper or e-magazine, however, the Back button has a very different action — it returns you to the article listing or the front page. E-newspaper and e-magazine content is sorted by articles or sections listings that you scroll through to select what you want to read. After reading an article, the Back button brings you back to the listing, not your Home screen.

In our personal experience, we use the Back button rarely when reading an e-book, but all the time when reading newspapers and magazines.

Kindle Store button

Next to the Back button is the Kindle Store button (it looks like a shopping cart). Tapping this button takes you to the Amazon Kindle Store. If wireless isn't turned on, you're prompted to activate it.

If you have a Wi-Fi only Kindle Touch and are not in an area with a Wi-Fi hotspot, you can't connect to the Kindle Store.

Search field

When you tap in the Search field, an onscreen keyboard appears. Type whatever you want to search for. A drop-down list lets you search My Items, Kindle Store, Wikipedia, or the Dictionary. Within an e-book, you can also restrict your search to just the e-book. Searching the Kindle Store or Wikipedia requires that Wi-Fi be turned on and connected.

Menu button

The Menu button is probably what you tap most often when using your Kindle Touch. We discuss specific uses of the Menu button throughout this e-book — turning on and off the wireless, finding the settings on your device, or reading annotations and notes. If you're wondering how to do something, no matter what it might be, tap the Menu button as your first choice. To close menus that appear onscreen, tap the X in the upper-right corner of the menu.

Text button

On the bottom toolbar, the Text button is labeled Aa. A number of useful features (see Figure 1-4) are accessed by pressing the Text button. Menu choices available from the Text button include

- ✔ **Style:** When you tap this option, you can make the following style settings:

    - *Font Size:* Change the text size. You can choose from eight sizes.

    - *Typeface:* Tap Regular, Condensed, Sans Serif to select your typeface.

- ✔ **Spacing:** When you tap this option, you can make the following spacing settings:

- *Line Spacing:* Tap Small, Medium, or Large to adjust the line spacing.

- *Words Per Line:* Change the number of words displayed per line. Your options include Fewest, Fewer, or Default.

Close the menu by tapping the X in the upper-right corner.

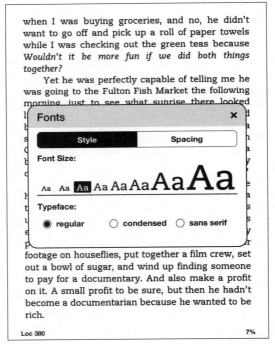

Figure 1-4: Press the Text button to change the font style and spacing.

Go To button

Tapping the Go To button on the bottom toolbar brings up a menu that allows you to quickly navigate through an e-book. You can go to the Cover, the *Beginning* (the first page of the first chapter), the Table of Contents (from here, tap and move to individual chapters), the *End* (the very last location in the book), or a specific page or location.

Sync or X-Ray button

The last button on the bottom toolbar is either Sync or X-Ray. *Sync* allows you to sync to the furthest page read. This is useful if you read an e-book on more than one device, such as your Kindle Touch and a smartphone. *X-Ray* displays if that feature is enabled in the book you're reading. Tapping X-Ray brings up a list of words or characters that appear in the page, chapter, or book along with a frequency graph.

If X-Ray is enabled in the book you're reading, you can still sync to the furthest page read. Just tap the Menu button — Sync is the third option in the list.

The Kindle display

Part of what made the Kindle so groundbreaking when it was introduced was that it was one of the first widely available commercial e-readers to use e-ink in its screen display. E-ink was first conceptualized by scientists at the Massachusetts Institute of Technology Media Lab; the e-ink corporation spun off and was founded in 1997.

E-ink is fundamentally different from an LCD screen, such as laptop, smartphone, and computer screens. With e-ink, thousands of microcapsules of ink are held between two layers of polymer. Reversing the electronic charge changes the capsules from positive to negative, which changes the color from light to dark and, ultimately, results in the display on the screen.

E-ink requires very little power, which is why the Kindle battery can hold a charge for up to a month if wireless is used minimally. E-ink isn't backlit, which is less fatiguing for your eyes; it also more closely mimics paper to enhance the reading experience. The drawback is that you need an external light source to read on the Kindle. On the plus side, you can read in bright sunlight without any glare.

Warning: The Kindle screen is delicate. Placing heavy objects on top of your Kindle, especially those with sharp edges, can damage the screen to the point that it's unreadable. Dropping your Kindle can also break the screen. Because of this, many people use covers and screen protectors to protect their Kindles. (See Chapter 5 for more about covers and other accessories.)

Toolbars in periodicals

Within a periodical, such as an e-newspaper or e-magazine, the toolbars are a little bit different, as shown in Figure 1-5. The top toolbar still contains the Back button, Search field, and Menu button, but it has two additional buttons:

- **Periodical Home button:** Displays the list of sections with photographs, as shown in Figure 1-5.

- **Sections and Articles button:** Displays a hierarchical, text-based section and article listing, as shown in Figure 1-6. At the bottom of the screen are navigation buttons.

Periodical Home button

Figure 1-5: The top toolbar of *The New York Times.*

Sections and Articles button

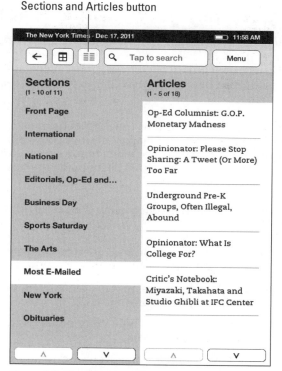

Figure 1-6: *The New York Times* displaying its text-based Sections and Articles listing.

 If you want to change the font size while reading a periodical, use the stretch/pinch motion. Stretch your fingers apart to enlarge the font, or pinch them together to make it smaller. Both of these actions are done on the touchscreen.

Making Your Kindle Touch Come Alive

After you open the box, you're ready to get started with your Kindle Touch and make it come alive. To do so, register your Kindle Touch, give it a name if you want, and set it up to receive e-mail. We describe each of these steps in the following sections.

Registering your Kindle Touch

If you bought your Kindle Touch for yourself through Amazon, it's delivered to you already registered. However, if you bought the Kindle Touch from a store (such as Target, Staples, or Best Buy) or received it as a gift, you need to register it.

You can register your Kindle Touch from the device itself or through your account at Amazon via your computer. The key piece of information you need when registering via a computer is the serial number, which can be found on the box or on the Device Info menu.

To register your Kindle Touch using the device, follow these steps:

1. **Make sure the wireless is on by tapping the Menu button and then selecting Turn On Wireless.**

2. **Once the wireless is on, tap Menu again, tap Settings and then tap Registration.**

3. **Enter your Amazon login credentials (your account e-mail and password).**

   The Kindle Touch inputs its own serial number, so you don't need to enter it.

4. **Tap Submit to finish registering your Kindle Touch.**

   That's it! You can now buy books and other content from Amazon and have them delivered wirelessly to your Kindle Touch.

To register your Kindle Touch from your Amazon account on your computer, follow these steps:

1. **Go to** www.amazon.com.

2. **Click the Your Account link in the upper-right corner.**

3. **From the main account page that appears, scroll down to the Digital Content section and then click the Manage Your Kindle link.**

4. **If prompted, enter your e-mail address and password, and then click the Sign In Using Our Secure Server button.**

5. **In the Serial Number text box, enter the serial number and click the Register a New Kindle button.**

   That's it! You can now buy e-books and other content and have them delivered wirelessly to your Kindle.

Naming your Kindle Touch

Naming your Kindle Touch is not required, but it's a way to be creative and make your Kindle uniquely yours. By default, your Kindle Touch is named *[Your Name]*'s Kindle. Its name appears in the upper-left corner of the Home screen. Similar to registering, you can change the name from the device or your Amazon account.

To change your Kindle Touch's name from the device, follow these steps:

1. **Tap the Menu button, tap Settings, tap Device Options.**

2. **Tap Device Name and enter a new name for your Kindle Touch using the on-screen keyboard that appears.**

   Some Kindle Touch owners use their name and phone number as their Kindle Touch's name. That way, if they misplace their Kindle Touch and a kind-hearted soul finds it, their name and contact information prominently displays on the Home screen.

3. **Tap the Save button to complete the process.**

To change the device name via your Amazon account on your computer, follow these steps:

1. **Go to** www.amazon.com.

2. **Click the Your Account link in the upper-right corner.**

3. **From the main account page that appears, scroll down to the Digital Content section and then click the Manage Your Kindle link.**

4. **If prompted, enter your e-mail address and password, and then click the Sign In Using Our Secure Server button.**

5. **Click on Manage Your Devices on the left side of the screen.**

   Your Kindle Touch appears on the list of registered devices.

6. **Click Edit next to the Kindle's name and then type a new name in the dialog box that appears.**

7. **Click the Update button.**

You can also add personal information or a message, such as "This Kindle Touch belongs to *[your name]*. If found, please call *xxx-xxx-xxx*." To do so, follow these steps:

1. **On the Kindle Touch, tap the Menu button, tap Settings, and then tap Personal Info.**

2. **Use the onscreen keyboard to enter the information.**

3. **Tap Save to complete the process.**

Note that when you "name" your Kindle with your name and phone number, it appears on the Home screen. If you include it in the personal information, it only appears on the Personal Info section of the Settings menu and won't be readily apparent to anyone who might happen to be looking at your Kindle Touch.

Setting the e-mail address on your Kindle Touch

Your Kindle Touch has an e-mail address, and with it, you can send personal documents to your device. If you buy books and don't want to sideload them to your Kindle Touch via the USB cable, you can simply e-mail them to your Kindle Touch. When you turn on wireless, any documents you e-mail to the device download and appear on your Home screen. (For more about loading your own documents on the Kindle Touch, see Chapter 4.)

The default Kindle Touch e-mail address is derived from the name on your Amazon account, followed by @kindle.com. You might want to change the e-mail address to something that's easier to remember or corresponds to the name you've given your Kindle Touch. To view your Kindle Touch's e-mail address, tap the Menu button and then tap Settings. The Send-to-Kindle E-mail option is the last item on the list. To change your Kindle Touch's e-mail address, you must do so from your Amazon account on your computer. Follow these steps:

1. **Go to** www.amazon.com.

2. **Click the Your Account link in the upper-right corner.**

3. **From the main account page that appears, scroll down to the Digital Content section and then click the Manage Your Kindle link.**

4. **If prompted, enter your e-mail address and password, and then click the Sign In Using Our Secure Server button.**

5. **From the left-hand menu, choose Personal Document Settings.**

   Your Kindle Touch and its associated e-mail address appear.

6. **Click Edit and input a new address.**

7. **Click the Update button to save.**

To send an e-mail to your Kindle Touch, you need to approve your own e-mail address and any others that might send content to your device. This can be done only through your Amazon account, not from the Kindle Touch.

To approve an e-mail address so it can send content to your Kindle Touch, follow these steps:

1. **Go to** www.amazon.com.

2. **Click the Your Account link in the upper-right corner.**

3. **From the main account page that appears, scroll down to the Digital Content section and then click the Manage Your Kindle link.**

4. **If prompted, enter your e-mail address and password, and then click the Sign In Using Our Secure Server button.**

5. **From the left-hand menu, choose Personal Document Settings.**

   The list of approved e-mail addresses is in the center of the screen.

6. **Click on Add a new approved e-mail address. Enter the e-mail address you want to approve in the dialog box that appears. Click Add Address when the information is complete. Repeat these steps to add and approve additional e-mail addresses.**

   The approved addresses are listed in the table in the center of the screen, with the option to delete them on the right (if you later choose to do so).

Many e-book retailers allow you to set up your account so that purchases you make are e-mailed automatically to your Kindle Touch. In essence, this mimics the wireless delivery service that Amazon offers. If you want to take advantage of this, make sure to add the e-mail address of the e-bookseller to your approved list of e-mail addresses.

If you use 3G to receive documents on your Kindle Touch 3G, Amazon charges $.15 per megabyte (within the U.S.) and $.99 per megabyte for Kindle Touches outside the U.S. The latter applies to a U.S.-registered Kindle Touch owner who's traveling outside the country, as well as non-U.S.-based Kindle owners. Transferring documents via Wi-Fi is free.

You can set the maximum document charge at your Amazon account. The range is $0–$49.50. The default maximum charge is $2.50. To change the amount, go to Personal Document Settings in your Amazon account and choose the option to edit the Whispernet Delivery charge (which can be found above the table of approved e-mail addresses).

Setting up your Wi-Fi

By default, all versions of the Kindle Touch include Wi-Fi; 3G is an additional option. If you have a Wi-Fi only Kindle Touch, you need to set up Wi-Fi to receive e-books and content wirelessly. If you have a Kindle Touch 3G, you don't have to set up Wi-Fi to receive content — 3G works automatically without any additional setup. Still, if you have a Wi-Fi hotspot in your home or office, you probably want to go ahead and get it working, just for convenience.

If you send documents to your Kindle Touch 3G via e-mail using 3G, there is a charge. Documents transferred via e-mail using Wi-Fi are free. Another good reason to set up Wi-Fi!

To set up Wi-Fi, you need to know whether the network is password-protected. This is probably the case in your home or office; Wi-Fi hotspots in public locations, such as Starbucks and McDonald's, are generally not secured with a password.

To add a wireless network, follow these steps:

1. **Make sure wireless is on by tapping the Menu button and then selecting Turn On Wireless.**

2. **Tap the Menu button again and then tap Settings.**

   Wi-Fi Networks is the second item on the list. See what networks (if any) the device has found.

3. **Tap Wi-Fi Networks, and in the menu that appears, select the network you want to connect to.**

   If the network you want to connect to requires a password, enter it in the Wi-Fi Networks dialog box that appears.

4. **(Optional) Manually enter a Wi-Fi network in the dialog box by following these steps:**

   a. *At the bottom of the Wi-Fi Networks box, tap Join to enter another Wi-Fi network. A dialog box named Enter Wi-Fi Network will appear, along with the on-screen keyboard.*

   b. *Enter the network name and if applicable, the password using the onscreen keyboard.*

   c. *At the bottom of the Enter Wi-Fi Network dialog box, tap the Advanced button.*

   You can advance through a series of screens using the up and down arrows. Each screen allows you to enter information relating to the network including connection type, IP address, and security type.

   d. *When all the necessary information has been entered, tap the Connect button to join the network.*

The wireless indicator displays in the upper-right corner of the screen next to the battery charge meter. The wireless indicator is visible from the Home screen, and you can see it every time you bring up the toolbar within an e-book. Icons you may see that relate to the wireless connection include

- **Wi-Fi:** The Kindle Touch is connected to a Wi-Fi network. Next to the words Wi-Fi is a fan with bars indicating the strength of the Wi-Fi connection

- **3G:** The Kindle Touch 3G is connected to a 3G network. This applies only to the Kindle Touch that includes 3G + Wi-Fi.

- **1X:** The Kindle Touch 3G is connected to a network via EDGE/GPRS (the predecessor to 3G in cellular network delivery). This applies only to the Kindle Touch 3G.

Understanding Kindle Touch Firmware

At the core of your Kindle Touch is a small computer, complete with hardware, software, and a built-in network platform. The software that runs the Kindle Touch is its firmware. *Firmware* is the core that controls how the device works — everything the Kindle Touch does is controlled by the firmware.

Amazon periodically updates the firmware for the device. Generally, firmware updates fix minor bugs and glitches that may not be apparent to the casual user. However, occasionally a major upgrade or new feature is added. For example, with firmware update 2.5, Amazon added the ability to sort e-books into collections, a feature that had been repeatedly requested by users.

To find out which version of the firmware your Kindle is running, from the Home screen, tap the Menu button, tap Settings, and then tap Menu again. Tap Device Info from the menu that appears. The firmware version is listed, along with the serial number, and space available (in megabytes). The Kindle Touch is the fifth generation of the devices that have been produced, so the firmware version begins with 5.

The firmware on your device may be updated automatically and not require any action from you. If an update is available, Your Kindle Touch will download it when you turn on the wireless and connect to a network. If you notice a screen that says Your Kindle is Updating, this is what's happening.

If you're curious whether a more current update is available, you can check at Amazon:

1. **Go to** www.amazon.com **and choose Kindle from the menu on the left side of the page and then choose Manage Your Kindle from the drop-down menu that appears.**

2. **On the taskbar near the top of the screen, click the Kindle Support link and then click the Kindle Software Updates link on the left side of the screen.**

3. **Instructions are included at the site for how todetermine if you need to upgrade the Firmware and if so, how to download and manually update your Kindle Touch, if you want.**

You don't have to manually update your Kindle Touch. Necessary updates happen automatically through the wireless. Just be aware that if the screen looks different or if you find new features, the device probably went through an automatic update.

Chapter 2

Reading on Your Kindle Touch

* *

In This Chapter

▶ Understanding your Kindle Touch's basic reading features

▶ Delving into additional helpful reading features

▶ Sharing what you're reading, and giving or lending e-books

▶ Managing your content

▶ Reading on other devices

* *

*I*n this chapter, we show you the basics of reading on your Kindle Touch — which is so simple and elegant that you'll soon forget you're even using an e-reader. Then we go into additional reading features — some that are very useful, and others that are just plain fun! Along the way, we share tips and hints that can save you time and make the most of your reading experience.

Getting to Know Your Kindle Touch's Reading Features

One of the reasons for the popularity of the Kindle family of e-readers is that the reading experience is so simple. Many first-time Kindle users express their delight in how easy it is to forget that they're even using an e-reader. The device disappears into the background and doesn't interfere with the pleasure of getting immersed in a good e-book.

That simple design approach is evident in Kindle Touch. Its intuitive touchscreen interface provides a non-intrusive way for you to immerse yourself in reading your e-books.

The following sections look at how to navigate through your collection of e-books and how to move around inside one.

Where it all begins: The Home screen

Your Kindle Touch's Home screen displays a list of all the content loaded on your Kindle Touch. Typically, that content is mostly e-books, but it can also include games, e-newspapers, e-magazines, blogs, and pictures.

When you first turn on your Kindle Touch (by pressing the power button on the bottom edge), it displays your last viewed page. No matter what displays, you can always go directly to your Home screen by pressing the Home button.

Your Home screen looks something like Figure 2-1. Note that Figure 2-1 shows the Home screen for a Kindle Touch with special offers, which have a small advertisement appearing near the bottom of the display.

Getting around the Home screen

When you first get your Kindle Touch, you may have only one page of content listed on your Home screen. You can easily open an e-book from the list by tapping anywhere in the row containing it.

As you add more e-books and other content, your Home screen can quickly become many pages long. After all, your Kindle Touch can hold about 3,000 e-books! It's amazing how quickly you can accumulate e-books, given how much free material is available and how easy it is to download them and other content to your Kindle Touch.

What's more, if you get in the habit of sampling e-books before you buy, your library of content can really start to grow! (We discuss sampling in Chapter 3.)

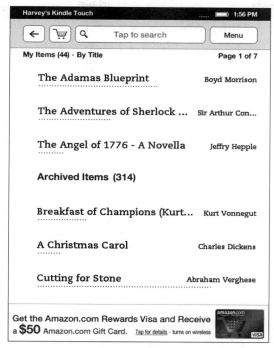

Figure 2-1: The Home screen lists all the content stored on your Kindle Touch.

So how do you manage your growing library of e-books? The following sections describe the features available from your Home screen that help you browse through your library and find e-books efficiently.

Sorting your e-books

The Home screen gives you options for sorting the content on your Kindle Touch. The current sorting method displays near the top center part of the screen. Your sorting options are Most Recent First, Title, Author, or Collections.

To change the sort option:

1. **Tap the displayed sort (for example, By Most Recent First) near the top center part of the screen.**

   A pop-up appears with different sort options.

2. **Tap your desired sort — Most Recent First, Title, Author, or Collections.**

   Presto! Your list of library content re-displays, sorted as you wish.

   Be sure to tap on the sort order, not My items which will pop up a different menu.

Don't worry if you don't have Collections set up yet. We discuss how to organize your content into collections in the "Managing Your E-Books and Other Content" section later in this chapter.

Paging through your Home screen

If your Home screen has multiple pages, you can flip forward and backward through those pages by swiping left (to move forward) or right (to move backward).

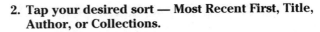

From the Home screen, you can navigate directly to a page in your list of e-books. Tap "Page x of y" near the top-right corner of the screen. A pop-up appears, allowing you to enter a page number to jump directly to in your list of content. If your Home screen is sorted by Title or by Most Recent First, you also have the option of entering the first few letters of a book's title. If your Home screen is sorted by Author, you can enter the first letters of an author. Tap the Go button and you're taken to the corresponding page in your list of content.

Finding that word

Another way to find an e-book loaded on your Kindle Touch is to search for it. The Kindle Touch has a powerful Search feature that scans all your content to find items containing a particular word or string of characters.

To search from the Home screen, tap the Search field located at the top center of the display. The onscreen keyboard appears.

When you tap in the Search field, My Items appears in the search box. By default, your Kindle Touch searches through the items in your library. You can change this by tapping the My Items option. A pop-up appears giving you the option to search My Items, Kindle Store, Wikipedia, or Dictionary.

Enter any text string by tapping the appropriate letters on the keyboard, and tap the Go button. Figure 2-2 shows the results of a search for *Rome.*

Figure 2-2: From the Home screen, you can search for words within all the content on your Kindle Touch.

Note the numbers in parentheses beside each title; those are the number of occurrences, or *hits,* of that search term in each e-book. By default, your search results are sorted by number of hits. Higher relevance is given to e-books with the search word in the title or with many occurrences of the word in the text.

You can change the order that your search options are sorted. Tap the current sort order — for example, By Number of Hits — to see all sort options, which include Number of Hits, Most Recent First, Title, and Author.

Selecting an e-book to read

Any of the methods discussed in the previous sections can be used to quickly find e-books from your Home screen. When you find the e-book you want to read, simply tap the displayed title to open it and begin reading.

Moving around in an e-book

Reading an e-book on a Kindle Touch is very intuitive. Tap pretty much anywhere on the page to go to the next page. (The "Next page" tap zone is the entire screen except for a ½-inch band along the left edge and a 1¼-inch band along the top edge. See Figure 1-2 in Chapter 1 for an illustration with measurements.) Tap near the left edge of the display to move back one page. To see a menu of options, tap near the top edge of the display.

As we note earlier, you can also swipe your finger left or right to page forward and backward, respectively, in the e-book.

You can also jump directly to various parts of an e-book. Tap near the top of the screen to bring up the toolbars. Different options are present on the toolbars that appear at the top and bottom of the display.

Tap the Go To button on the toolbar at the bottom of the screen. A pop-up window appears, similar to the window shown in Figure 2-3. The list of options may differ for different e-books; for example, not all e-books have a defined Table of Contents or a cover.

The list here shows the Go To options you may see:

- ✔ **Cover:** Jumps to the cover of the e-book.
- ✔ **Beginning:** Moves to the first text in the e-book.
- ✔ **Table of Contents:** Jumps to the Table of Contents, where you can select a particular chapter to move to.
- ✔ **End:** Jumps to the end of the e-book.
- ✔ **Page or Location:** Moves to a particular page or location in the e-book. We discuss the concept of *page* and *location* as it pertains to e-books shortly.

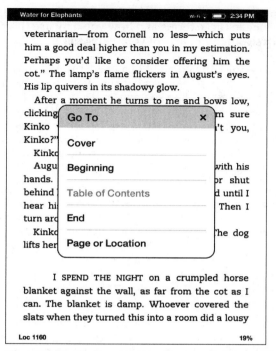

Figure 2-3: The Go To menu lets you move directly to different sections of the e-book.

As you read, the area at the bottom of the screen displays your location in the e-book, with a location number for the text currently in view and a percentage indicating how far into the e-book you've read.

When you first open an e-book, your Kindle Touch displays the title, connectivity information (3G or Wi-Fi), battery charge, and time of day at the top of the screen. As you page ahead, it removes this display to show you more of your e-book's text. If you want to see this again at any time, tap the top of the screen to bring up this information along with the toolbars.

When you tap the Page or Location option from the Go To pop-up window, you can enter a desired page number or a location in the e-book. Some e-books don't have the Page option, but all have the Location option. Time to dig into the difference in these terms and how you may use them to reference different parts of your e-book:

- **Location:** The concept of a fixed, printed "page" doesn't really apply to e-books because you can vary the font type, font size, line spacing, and words per line. All those changes affect how much of the e-book displays on a given screen. So, e-books use *locations* to describe where you are in it. A *location* within an e-book remains constant even if the screen or font size changes. As you read an e-book, your current location displays, and it changes as you move through it.

- **Page number:** For many e-books, your Kindle Touch also displays a page number. The displayed page number reflects the page number in the printed edition of the book that corresponds to your current location. This is helpful, for example, if you're reading an e-book in a reading group in which some members use Kindles and others use printed copies of the book; you can all turn to a particular page.

Even for books that have page information, the display shows only current location, and percentage completed, as you page through the book. You can view the current page number at any time by touching the top of the screen, and the current page will display on the bottom toolbar.

Although all e-books have location information, not all e-books have page numbers. For example, if a book exists only in e-book form and hasn't been published in a print version, no page numbers are available.

A *location* is simply a marker indicating how far you are in the e-book; it's equivalent to 128 bytes of information in the e-book file.

Zooming in on pictures

Kindle Touch e-books may include graphics and pictures as well as text. To zoom in on those pictures:

1. **Tap and hold the graphic.**

   A magnifying glass icon appears in the graphic.

2. **Tap the magnifying glass to zoom in on the image.**

   The image expands and may rotate to fill the available use of the display.

3. **Tap the image again to return to the content.**

Going beyond the Basics with Helpful Reading Features

In the following sections, we get into some ways the Kindle Touch can enhance your reading experience. These features give you the power to adjust the Kindle Touch display, listen to an e-book with Text-to-Speech, look up words, highlight text, make notes, post on Facebook and Twitter with e-book excerpts and ratings, and much more.

Easy dictionary look-up

One of the most useful Kindle Touch features is the built-in dictionary. The dictionary is easy to access and makes it swift and painless to instantly bring up the definition of the word.

To bring up a dictionary definition for a word, just tap and hold the word. The selected word is highlighted — in other words, it displays with white text on black background. When you release your finger, a short dictionary definition for the word appears onscreen in a pop-up box. To clear the definition, tap anywhere outside the pop-up box.

If you want to know more, tap the Show Full Definition button, and a dictionary page opens with the full dictionary information for the word. Press the Back button in the top-left corner to return to your text.

The Kindle Touch's default dictionary is the *New Oxford American Dictionary* (Oxford University Press), which is included with your Kindle Touch. You can select a different dictionary to be the default by following these steps:

1. **Press the Home button to bring up the Home screen.**

2. **Tap the Menu button, tap the Settings option, and then tap the Dictionaries setting.**

   The active dictionary displays.

3. **Tap the active dictionary to change to a different dictionary.**

   A list of available dictionaries displays.

4. **Select a different dictionary by tapping the selection button beside it.**

Two dictionaries are provided with your Kindle Touch: the *New Oxford American Dictionary* and the *Oxford Dictionary of English* (Oxford University Press). Additional dictionaries can be purchased from the Kindle Store; be sure the dictionary indicates that it's a Kindle-supported dictionary in order to use it as your default dictionary.

Utilizing highlights and notes

As you're reading, you may want to highlight text to refer to later or add your own notes to a particular passage. You may even want to make a Facebook post or Twitter tweet that includes an excerpt from the e-book. The touchscreen makes it particularly convenient for you to make these marks, or *annotations:*

 ✓ **Highlights** shade a section of text to draw attention to it.

 ✓ **Notes** are the text you type, much like when you jot notes in the margins of a printed book.

All these annotations are stored on your Kindle Touch and are backed up at Amazon. This enables you to recover your annotations if you lose your Kindle Touch or upgrade to another model.

To make these annotations, select text in your e-book by touching your finger to a word and dragging it across the screen. As you do so, selected text appears as white text on black background.

When you release your finger, a pop-up window provides buttons: Highlight, Add Note, or Share. In the following sections, we look at each option.

Annotating is disabled in e-book samples; you can't add notes, highlights, or bookmarks, or share excerpts, when viewing an e-book sample.

Highlighting text

With the desired text selected (see the preceding section), tap the Highlight button. The text is highlighted in the e-book — appearing as white text on a black background.

To delete a highlight, select any of the highlighted words by touching and dragging across them. A Delete button appears in a pop-up window; tap it to remove the highlight.

What if the text you want to highlight spans more than one page? You can adjust the font size to get all of your desired text on the screen. Or, you can adjust the starting point of the displayed text by changing the location. Touch the top of the screen to bring up the Menu, tap the Go To button, and tap Page or Location. Enter a location slightly different than the current location to shift the starting point of the displayed text, until all of your desired text is displayed.

An interesting thing about highlights is that you can view highlights that *other readers* have made. Amazon collects this information and highlights passages in your e-book that have been highlighted frequently by other readers. Your Kindle Touch displays how many people have highlighted that particular passage.

Although this can be intriguing, some readers find the display of popular highlights distracting. To turn off these popular highlights, follow these steps:

1. **From the Home screen, tap the Menu button, tap Settings, and then tap Reading Options.**

   Popular Highlights is one of the Reading Options listed.

2. Tap the On/Off toggle button to deactivate the Popular Highlights option.

If you don't want to share your highlighted passages with Amazon, turn off the Annotations Backup option in the Reading Options page under Settings. If you do this, your various annotations aren't backed up by Amazon, and they won't display on other devices registered to your Amazon account.

Taking notes

Want to make margin notes in your e-books? Well, you can with your Kindle Touch. Adding notes is similar to making highlights.

With the desired text selected, as we describe in the "Utilizing highlights and notes" section earlier in this chapter, tap the Add Note button. A pop-up window appears with a text entry block and the onscreen keyboard. Type your notes via the keyboard and tap the Save button when complete.

Notice that the text associated with your note is now highlighted in your e-book and is followed by a superscripted number. Tapping that number brings up your note's text block — where you can edit or delete it.

Viewing annotations

You can view all your notes, highlights, and bookmarks for a particular e-book. While reading an e-book, tap the top of the screen to bring up the toolbar. Tap the Menu button, and then tap View Notes & Marks. All your notes, your highlights, and the popular highlights for that e-book display.

You can also view all your annotations across all your e-books, e-magazines, e-newspapers, and personal documents. Kindle Touch places those in a My Clippings file that's available as a document from your Home screen. You can read your My Clippings file just as you would any other document on your Kindle Touch.

You can also use an Amazon web page to view your annotations from a personal computer: `http://kindle.amazon.com` (U.S. and other countries) or `http://kindle.amazon.co.uk` (U.K.).

Sharing highlights and notes with Twitter and Facebook

You probably noticed that when creating or viewing highlights and notes in your e-book, a Share button is available. This button lets you share a note, and a link to the selected passage, through social media sites, such as Facebook and Twitter. You can do all this directly from your Kindle Touch — no computer required! This Share button is a fun way to let others know about e-books you're enjoying.

When you use your Kindle Touch to share on Twitter, your tweet consists of your short note plus a Kindle Store link to the e-book you're reading. Figure 2-4 shows sample tweets on Twitter after being created on a Kindle Touch.

Figure 2-4: You can tweet about your e-books right from your Kindle Touch.

From your Kindle Touch, you can also update your Facebook page with an e-book cover image, an excerpt of highlighted text, and a note. Figure 2-5 shows a Facebook status update created from a Kindle Touch.

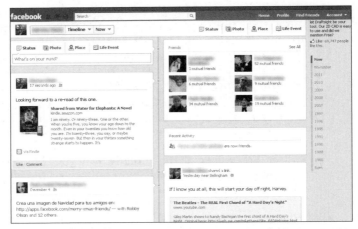

Figure 2-5: A Facebook status update created from a Kindle Touch with a link to the e-book.

To take advantage of these features, you need to link your Kindle Touch with your Twitter and/or Facebook accounts. To do so, follow these steps:

1. **From the Kindle Touch's Home screen, tap the Menu button, tap Settings, and then tap Reading Options.**

2. **Tap Social Networks. (If wireless is off, you're prompted to turn it on.)**

   A screen similar to Figure 2-6 appears. From here you can tell your Kindle Touch the usernames and passwords associated with your accounts.

3a. **To link to your Twitter account, tap the Link Account button for Twitter; enter your Twitter e-mail address and your Twitter password on the authorization screen that appears.**

3b. **To link to your Facebook account, tap the Link Account button for Facebook; enter your e-mail address and Facebook password on the authorization screen that appears.**

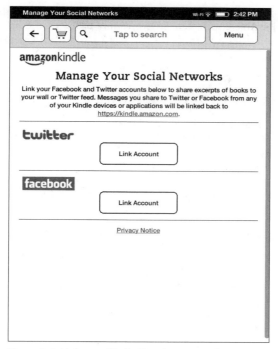

Figure 2-6: Link your Kindle Touch to your social accounts to share information.

After your Kindle Touch is linked, you can share a note about what you're reading by following these steps:

1. **From within an e-book, select text by sliding your finger across the page.**

2. **Tap the Share button.**

3. **Enter your message in the text box that appears and then tap Share again.**

   Your note and a link to the selected e-book passage posts to the accounts — Twitter, Facebook, or both — that you have linked to your Kindle Touch.

You can share Twitter and Facebook updates not only for e-books that you're reading, but also for periodicals and your personal documents. (You can read more about personal documents in Chapter 4.)

More toolbar options

When reading an e-book, menu options are available with useful features for accessing while you're reading. Tap the top of the screen, and tap the Menu button in the top-right corner of the display.

From within an e-book, the Menu button includes the options we discuss in the following sections.

Turn On/Off Wireless

Leaving wireless turned on allows you to automatically receive updates, such as recently purchased e-books, subscriptions, and popular highlights, from the Kindle Store. You may want to turn off wireless when you want to prolong battery life or when using your Kindle Touch on airplanes when wireless may not be allowed.

Kindle Touch with Wi-Fi and 3G: On an airplane, 3G must *always* be turned off.

Shop in Kindle Store

This option brings up the Kindle Store for you to browse and find e-books.

Sync to Furthest Page Read

If the e-book you're reading has been viewed by you (or others on your Amazon account) on other devices, you can adjust your location to the furthest page read in the e-book with this option.

Book Description

This option displays the e-book's description from the Kindle Store. You need wireless turned on to view the e-book's description, so you're prompted to turn it on, if necessary.

Add Bookmark

Want to save a particular location in an e-book? Tap this option to bookmark it! You can place a bookmark at any location, and you can have multiple bookmarks in an e-book. You can tell whether your current location is bookmarked by the little dog-ear icon that appears in the top-right corner of the display.

If the location has already been bookmarked, the Add Bookmark option changes to Delete the bookmark.

View Notes & Marks

Tapping this option displays your highlighted sections, your notes, and your bookmarks for the current e-book. Popular highlights from other readers also display.

Turn On Text-to-Speech

Your Kindle Touch can read aloud to you! Tap this option, and your Kindle reads aloud from the current page; it automatically turns pages as it reads the e-book. The sound plays through the Kindle Touch's speakers. If you prefer, you can plug earphones into the Kindle Touch's headphone jack instead.

To turn off Text-to-Speech, tap anywhere on the screen and then tap the Off button in the lower-right corner.

While Text-to-Speech is active, you can tap the screen to view an audio control bar that allows you to slow down or speed up the speech. You can also change the voice from the default male voice to a female voice, adjust the volume, and turn off Text-to-Speech from the control bar.

Text-to-Speech isn't available for all e-books; the availability of this feature is controlled by the e-book's publisher. However, most e-books, e-newspapers, e-magazines, blogs, or any personal documents you load have this feature enabled. The Amazon product page for an e-book will specify Text-to-Speech: Enabled for e-books that have the feature enabled.

If you want your Kindle Touch to turn pages automatically while you read, turn on Text-to-Speech, but turn the Volume control all the way down. Then adjust the font size so that the automatic page turns are at a comfortable reading pace. This comes in handy, for example, when using your Kindle Touch when you're working out on a treadmill.

Text button

As we describe in Chapter 1, this button can be used to change the font size, typeface, line spacing, and words per line.

X-Ray

Some e-books have the X-Ray feature enabled. This new feature provides a view into the recurring items of the e-book: characters, settings, topics, and phrases that occur throughout it. You can view this information for the current page, the current chapter, or the entire e-book. Tap any term to bring up additional information from Wikipedia and from Shelfari, a community-driven website for collecting and sharing book information.

Lending, Library Borrowing, and Gifting E-Books

Innovative features are available for your Kindle Touch that give you new ways to lend e-books to others, borrow from libraries, and give e-books as gifts.

Lending e-books

You can loan an e-book to anyone — even if they don't have a Kindle! All you need is the person's e-mail address.

You can loan e-books from your computer. Follow these steps to lend an e-book to a friend:

1. **Open a web browser on your personal computer and go to the Manage Your Kindle page (www.amazon. com/myk).**

   If you're not already logged in, you're prompted to do so.

2. **Scroll down to view the e-books in your Kindle library.**

3. **Hover over the Actions button for an e-book.**

   If lending has been enabled for the e-book, a Loan This Title option appears.

4. **Click the Loan This Title option, and on the page that appears, enter the person's e-mail address, name, and a message.**

   The borrower of the e-book receives an e-mail from Amazon, similar to the message in Figure 2-7. The borrower has seven days to accept the loan by clicking the Get Your Loaned Book Now button provided in the e-mail.

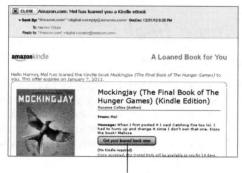

Click this button to accept the loan

Figure 2-7: When you lend an e-book, Amazon sends an e-mail to the borrower.

What if the person you've loaned the e-book to doesn't have a Kindle? No problem! You can use many devices to read Kindle e-books. In the "Reading Any Time, Anywhere on Other Devices" section later in this chapter, we explore different devices that can be used to read Kindle e-books.

The borrower can return the loaned e-book before the 14-day loan is over. To return a borrowed Kindle e-book, go to the Your Orders section of the Manage Your Kindle page on Amazon. Click the plus symbol (+) next to the loaned title and then click the Delete This Title link.

Currently, only e-book customers residing in the U.S. can lend Kindle e-books. Loans can be made to people living outside the U.S., but the borrower may not be able to accept the loan, depending on geographic differences in publishing rights.

You can join Kindle community forums to participate in exchanges in which Kindle owners lend and borrow e-books. A popular one can be found at KindleBoards — click the Lend and Borrow Exchange link at `www.kindleboards.com`.

Want to know if a book is lendable before you purchase it? From a personal computer, view the book's product page on Amazon. Scroll down to the Product Details section and look for Lending: Enabled.

While an e-book from your Kindle is on loan, you can't read it.

Borrowing e-books from the library

Many public libraries allow Kindle e-books to be checked out. How does this work? The e-book is made available to you for a fixed amount of time — the loan period varies by library — and then it expires. When the loan expires, the e-book is no longer available to you, unless you check it out again or purchase it from Amazon's Kindle Store.

You can make highlights, notes, and bookmarks in a borrowed library e-book. Those annotations are preserved even after the e-book loan expires, if you later decide to purchase the e-book or borrow it again.

To borrow e-books, go to your local public library's website. If your library supports OverDrive digital e-book services, you can check out Kindle-compatible e-books. Note that you have to use your library card, just as you would when borrowing a printed book.

Public library e-books for Kindle e-readers are presently available only in the United States.

From your library's website, you can have the e-book delivered wirelessly to your Kindle. If you haven't received a checked-out e-book on your Kindle, it may be because you don't have Wi-Fi activated. Library e-books are sent wirelessly only through Wi-Fi; they are not distributed over a 3G connection.

Gifting e-books

You can give anyone an e-book from the e-book's product page on Amazon. A Give as a Gift button is available for most e-books in the Kindle Store.

You can e-mail the gift directly to someone and specify when the e-mail should be sent. The recipient receives a link in the e-mail that enables them to access the e-book.

Alternatively, you can have the e-mail sent to you. You may wish to do this if you want to forward the e-mail later to the giftee, or if you prefer to print the e-mail and present the gift that way.

Many online e-booksellers also let you give an e-book as a gift, too. Details on how to do so will be available at the seller's website. We list some popular e-booksellers in the "Checking Out Other Online Stores" section in Chapter 3.

Managing Your E-Books and Other Content

As you use your Kindle Touch, you'll likely deal with a long and growing list of e-books and other content on your device. Putting your fingers on specific content can be challenging when you have hundreds of items loaded on your Kindle Touch, spread across dozens of pages.

Kindle Touch helps organize this cornucopia of content with collections. You can create various collections and assign your e-books to them to help organize your content. For example, you might put all the e-books that you've finished reading into a Finished collection. Or if you want to keep track of all e-books you've read in a given year, you could create a Finished in 2011 collection. You could put your dictionaries and product manuals into a References collection. And you might set up different collections for your favorite genres: Paranormal, Romance, Horror, Biographies, and so on. You can set up any type of collection you can think of!

By grouping your Kindle e-books and other content into collections, it can be easier to find specific items when you want them. To create a collection, follow these steps:

1. **From the Home screen, tap the Menu button, and then tap Create New Collection.**

   A pop-up window appears.

2. **In the pop-up window, enter a name for the new collection using the onscreen keyboard.**

Adding an e-book to a collection is similarly straightforward:

1. **From the Home screen, tap and hold the name of the e-book.**

   A set of options appears.

2. **Tap Add to Collection and then select the collection you want to add the e-book to.**

 You can assign an e-book to more than one collection. You might put an e-book into a Finished collection and a Biographies collection to label the genre, for example.

 You might be surprised to see your e-book appear on your Home screen list after you move it to a collection. This behavior depends on the sort option you've selected for your Home screen. When your Home screen sorts by title, the collections are listed along with all e-books on your Kindle Touch, alphabetically. If you change to sort by collections, your collections display in alphabetical order at the top of your Home screen, followed by any e-books and other content that aren't assigned to a collection. (See the "Sorting your e-books" section, earlier in this chapter, for details on sorting your Kindle content.)

Reading Any Time, Anywhere on Other Devices

E-books purchased from the Kindle Store can be read on your Kindle Touch, of course, but they can also be read on many other devices. Amazon has made free Kindle reading applications that can be used to read Kindle-compatible e-books even by people who don't own a Kindle e-reader. These applications can also be used by you to read your e-books when your Kindle Touch isn't handy.

Kindle e-books can be read using the free Kindle reading apps for the following devices:

- PC
- Mac
- iPad
- iPhone
- Android
- Windows Phone
- BlackBerry
- WebOS

This list of supported devices is likely to grow over time. You can see a current list of supported devices on the Kindle Support page (www.amazon.com/gp/help/customer/display.html/ref=sv_kinc_9?ie=UTF8&nodeId=200127470).

From the Kindle Support page, click the Kindle Reading Applications link to see the different devices for which a Kindle reading application is available.

To read Kindle e-books on other devices, you need to register those devices to your account. Do so from the Manage Your Kindle page (www.amazon.com/myk). You're prompted to sign in if you haven't already done so. Click the Manage Your Devices link in the left column of the page. Scroll down to the Registered Kindle Reading App section for instructions for your particular device.

If you've started reading an e-book on one device and then resume reading on another device, you can position yourself at the last page read in the e-book. This is done through the magic of *Whispersync,* which is Amazon's technology for keeping your reading synchronized among the different devices you use. Whispersync makes it possible to continue reading seamlessly on whatever device is handiest for you at any time.

Whispersync works across all devices registered to the same Amazon account. It synchronizes the furthest page read and any bookmarks, notes, and highlights. Remember that for the synchronization to take place, wireless must be turned on in each of the devices to be synced.

You can turn off the Whispersync synchronization if you wish. Do this from the Manage Your Kindle page on Amazon (www.amazon.com/myk). Click **Manage Your Devices** in the left column. The Device Synchronization area provides a link where you can turn off or turn on synchronization.

Do you want to capture a screenshot of what's displayed on your Kindle Touch screen? You can! Press and hold the Home button and tap the screen. Hold the button for another second or two and let go. A graphics file in GIF format is stored on your Kindle Touch's root directory. To transfer that file to your personal computer, connect your Kindle Touch to the computer with its USB cable. Your Kindle Touch appears as an external drive, with the screenshots in the main (root) directory of the drive. You can view those files directly, or drag and drop them to a folder on your personal computer.

Chapter 3

Finding Content for Your Kindle Touch

*Y*ou're holding your Kindle Touch in your hands — it's registered, charged, and ready to go. What do you want to do? Read, of course! But to make that happen, you need to have content on your Kindle Touch, whether that's an e-book, e-newspaper, e-magazine, blog, or something else. Although the way the wireless service downloads content to your Kindle Touch seems almost magical, you need to initiate the process. This chapter discusses finding content — from e-books to blogs and everything in between — and how to get the treasures you find onto your Kindle Touch in the easiest way possible.

Starting Your Search in the Kindle Store

The fastest, easiest, and most convenient place to find Kindle Touch content is at the Amazon Kindle Store, which makes sense, of course, because Amazon invented the device.

One common misconception is that you have to buy *all* Kindle content from Amazon. This isn't true. Although Amazon makes shopping for Kindle Touch content remarkably simple, you can find plenty of other online stores that sell Kindle-compatible e-books, as we discuss later in this chapter in the "Checking Out Other Online Stores" section.

Searching and browsing for e-books on your computer

Amazon has a specific Kindle Store that makes it easy to search for Kindle Touch content. Go to www.amazon.com and from the Search drop-down list, choose Kindle Store to restrict your search to Kindle-specific content, as shown in Figure 3-1.

Select this option

Enter the search term here

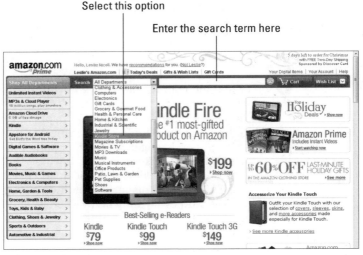

Figure 3-1: Restricting your search to the Kindle Store.

In the Search field, type the words for your search. Do you have a specific e-book in mind? Type the title, or even just a few words of the title. Are you looking for e-books by a particular author? Type the author's name. Are you interested in deep sea diving — or any other subject that tickles your fancy? Type a few words, click the Go button to the right of the Search field, and *voilà!* If anything is in the store, it appears in the search results. With 1,137,635 Kindle-compatible e-books in the store (as of this writing), something will probably appear!

Just for fun, we entered **archery** and received an interesting assortment of results (277 in all): a variety of non-fiction e-books including a history of bows and arrows; how to make a crossbow; how to *fletch* (or put feathers on) arrows; the Zen of archery; Kyudo, the Japanese art of archery; a business plan for an archery store; and novels such as *Robin Hood and the Bells of London (Clayton Emery's Tales of Robin Hood)* by Clayton Emery.

If you're more of a browser, less of a searcher, Amazon makes that easy, too. After you choose the Kindle Store, a bar appears below the search bar and lists the departments in the Kindle Store:

- ✔ Buy a Kindle
- ✔ Free Reading Apps
- ✔ Kindle eBooks
- ✔ Kindle Singles
- ✔ Newsstand
- ✔ Popular Games
- ✔ Accessories
- ✔ Discussions
- ✔ Manage Your Kindle
- ✔ Kindle Support

One frequently asked question at KindleBoards is "How do I contact Kindle support?" Support is just a click away at the Kindle Store; just click the Kindle Support link on the search bar, as shown in Figure 3-2.

Click the Kindle eBooks link, and you land on a page that should happily satisfy your browsing dreams. In the center of the page are lists such as New & Noteworthy, Kindle Singles, Picks for You, and other options (note that this page changes frequently) with the e-book covers prominently featured. The left side of the page includes Book Deals, Popular Features (such as *The New York Times* Best Sellers), and Categories for searching specific topic areas. This allows you to drill down a bit more while browsing. Gay & Lesbian? Travel? Click the link, and you're presented with a plethora of choices to capture your fancy. The right side of the page shows two lists that are updated hourly: Top 100 Paid and Top 100 Free, as well as the Kindle Daily Deal.

Click this link

Figure 3-2: Click the Kindle Support link to find help.

Even though over a million Kindle-compatible e-books are in the Kindle Store, still millions upon millions of printed books are in the world. Unfortunately, they aren't all available in a Kindle edition. If a particular book you want is for sale at Amazon (U.S.) in print form, but not in a Kindle version, click the Tell the Publisher! I'd Like to Read This Book on Kindle link on the book's product page. Does clicking the link make a difference? We suspect that it does. For example, popular author John Grisham was originally opposed to e-books, but his entire backlist became available for purchase in the Kindle Store in late 2010. Consumer demand likely influenced this change.

Searching and browsing for e-books on your Kindle Touch

"Wait a minute!" we hear you saying, "I don't want to use my computer to search for e-books. Can I do this from my Kindle Touch?" Of course you can! The first step is to turn on the wireless by tapping the top of the screen to bring up the toolbar (if you are in a book. No need to do this from the Home screen as the toolbar is always visible). Tap the Menu button and select Turn On Wireless. If your Kindle Touch is in Sleep mode, wake it up by pressing the power button.

If you have a Wi-Fi only Kindle Touch, you need to be somewhere with a Wi-Fi hotspot. If you have a Kindle Touch 3G, you should be good to go anywhere that has 3G service.

When the wireless is on and has a good connection, tap the Shop in Kindle store button (the one that looks like a shopping cart). Alternatively, you can tap the Menu button and select Shop in Kindle Store. Either way, you see a page similar to the one shown in Figure 3-3. At the top, you have the option to browse Books, Newspapers, Magazines, Audible Audiobooks, Kindle Singles, and Blogs. As you move down the page, you can browse *NY Times* Best Sellers, Kindle Best Sellers, 100 Books, $3.99 or Less, the Kindle Daily Post, Popular Games and Things to Try. The Recommended for You section features e-books that might be of particular interest to you, based on your prior purchases. The more you buy from Amazon, the more tailored the recommendations are.

To exit the store, press the Home button on your Kindle Touch. You can also return to your Home screen by tapping the Back arrow (upper-left corner of the toolbar). Remember to turn off wireless to conserve the battery.

Getting a taste before you commit: Sampling content

When you find an e-book that intrigues you, you can send a sample to your Kindle Touch to decide whether you really want to purchase it. *Samples* consist of the first ten percent of the e-book, which is usually enough to give you a flavor of the writing. Sampling isn't perfect, however; sometimes the first ten percent of an e-book is mostly the *front matter* (Table of Contents, Foreword, Acknowledgements, and so on), and you never get to the good stuff. If that's the case, it will likely deter you from buying the e-book! However, based on our experience, this is becoming less of a problem than it was in the early days of Kindle e-books. Publishers seem to be aware of the issue and are formatting their e-books so that relevant content is included in the sample, allowing a potential buyer to make an informed purchase decision.

Figure 3-3: Browse for e-books and more from your Kindle Touch.

Sampling e-books on multiple devices

You can have multiple Kindles as well as other devices running the Kindle application (PCs, smartphones, and so on) registered to your Kindle account. You can register a new Kindle Touch either from the device or from your computer via your Amazon account (see Chapter 1 to find out how to register your Kindle Touch). To register other devices, download the Kindle app and register using the device. More details on this process can be found at

```
www.amazon.com/gp/help/customer/display.
     html/ref=hp_200127470_ksupport_
     mobile?nodeId=200783640
```

If you search or browse for Kindle content from your computer, you can send a sample to any of the devices registered to your Kindle account, including devices that run the Kindle app, such as the iPhone, a BlackBerry, or other PCs. If you search for content on your Kindle Touch, you can send a sample only to the Kindle on which you're doing the searching.

If you enjoy the sample and want to buy the e-book, you have two options to do so. One is to tap at the top of the screen to bring up the toolbar and then tap the Menu button. On the list that appears, tap the Buy This Book Now option (see Figure 3-4). Alternatively, when you reach the end of the sample, you can purchase the e-book. Figure 3-5 shows the screen that you see to make a purchase at the end of the e-book — just tap the Buy Now link to purchase it. In either case, make sure that wireless is on.

Tap this option

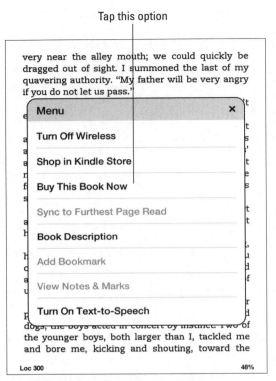

Figure 3-4: Buy the e-book via the Menu button.

When you tap the Buy This Book Now option (from the Menu button) or the Buy Now link (at the end of the e-book sample), you're taken to the e-book's product page at Amazon. Even though you see this page, you can't browse — the purchase is made immediately, and your account is charged. If you tap the Buy This Book Now option or the Buy Now link by mistake, you can cancel the purchase on the next screen that appears, asking if you bought the book by accident. If you want to verify the price before buying the e-book, tap the Book Description option from the Menu button or the See Details for This Book in the Kindle Store link at the end of the e-book sample. Then, while in the Kindle Store, you can buy the e-book if you wish.

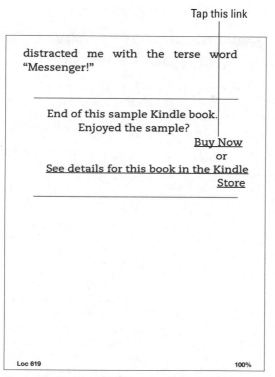

Figure 3-5: Buy the e-book when you finish the sample.

When you reach the end of the sample, make note of the location number. Then, if you choose to purchase the e-book, you can open it and use the Go To feature to travel to that specific location and resume reading where you left off. Unfortunately, e-books and samples don't synchronize with each other, so when you open your newly purchased e-book, you'll be at the beginning. Knowing the location number allows you to navigate quickly through the e-book and pick right up where you left off.

Lending versus sharing Kindle e-books and other content

When you purchase Kindle e-books from Amazon, they're associated with your Amazon account. If you have more than one Kindle device or app registered to your account, content can be *shared* among the devices, but it can't be shared with a device or app registered to another account. Sharing refers specifically to "sharing" books among devices registered to a single Amazon account. While you might not mind having multiple devices on your account, keep in mind that those other devices — and their users — have access to your account to buy content using the credit card associated with the account. Even though devices on the same account can be shared, publishers may limit how many times you can download a copy simultaneously to different devices or apps. Books do not have unlimited sharing privileges.

Some Kindle e-books can be loaned to devices not registered to your account. In general, e-books that can be loaned to another Kindle owner on a different account can be lent only once, for a period of two weeks. While the e-book is on loan, it isn't available to you. (Read more about lending e-books — as well as borrowing e-books from public libraries offering titles in the Kindle format — in Chapter 2.)

Current subscription content, such as e-magazines and e-newspapers, are limited to one Kindle at a time, that is, two people could not "share" a daily subscription to the New York Times and read the current day paper at the same time. Past issues can be downloaded to compatible devices on the same account. Subscription content cannot be loaned across accounts.

If you give a used Kindle as a gift, the content you purchased can't be given as a gift. The device must be deregistered and previous content erased. You can deregister a Kindle Touch on the device itself (in the settings section) or from the Manage Your Devices section of your Amazon account. Follow the same steps as you did to register your Kindle Touch; the options will change to "deregister" instead (see Chapter 1 for instructions on how to register your device).

Read the License Agreement and Terms of Use at the Kindle Store. This document governs the use of e-books and digital content you download from Amazon. It can be found at www.amazon.com/kindlelicense.

You can't buy e-books or other content from your Kindle Touch without a wireless connection, either Wi-Fi or 3G. On the other hand, if you buy an e-book while browsing on your PC and send it to your Kindle, that purchase is queued and sent to your Kindle the next time you turn on wireless, whether it be minutes, days, or weeks later.

Locating superior subscription content

Kindle content isn't restricted to just e-books. In fact, one of the earliest selling points of the device was the ability to subscribe to Kindle versions of popular magazines, newspapers, and blogs. This type of content has been steadily increasing over the years, and at present, several hundred magazines, newspapers, and blogs are available.

You have two options available for acquiring this type of content — an ongoing subscription or the purchase of a single issue. Per issue prices for a subscription will be less than the price to purchase a single issue, and both will *usually* be less than a traditional subscription or a print purchase. We say *usually* because you may find a bargain or deeply discounted subscription price that would be less than a Kindle subscription. If price is the determining factor, do your homework and shop around. On the other hand, if decreasing the clutter in your home is important and you want the convenience of wireless delivery daily, weekly, or monthly, you may find that a Kindle subscription is a viable option.

Some subscription content is available for free online, such as certain newspapers. So why pay for a Kindle Touch subscription? If you commute on a train or a bus, the convenience of having the paper on your Kindle Touch might be the deciding factor. On the other hand, if you like to read the paper on your computer, a subscription might not be a smart purchase. Keep in mind that Kindle subscriptions don't include advertising, whereas online periodicals often do.

All Kindle subscriptions come with a 14-day free trial, at minimum. Special promotions may be offered with 90-day free trials for subscription content. You can cancel any time during the trial whether it be 14 days or 90. If you don't cancel, your subscription begins automatically at the end of the trial period. Of course, you can cancel a subscription at any time, even after subscribing; you'll receive a pro-rated refund on the unused portion of your subscription. Please note that the trial (14 or 90 days) is a one-time option — if you cancel and then decide later you want to subscribe, even if many months have gone by, your new paid subscription starts immediately.

Kindle subscriptions can be confusing because there are lots of little quirks that are generally not an issue with e-books. Recognize that many of these exist because of the way the publisher has decided to format and distribute the content, and thus these issues are not under the control of Amazon. Here are some things to be aware of:

- ✔ **The Kindle Touch is a grayscale device.** Magazines and newspapers that rely heavily on color photographs don't look the same on the Kindle Touch. It may not be a pleasurable reading experience for you for this reason.

- ✔ **Content that's included in the print edition may not be included in the Kindle subscription version.** For example, *The New Yorker* doesn't include its full complement of cartoons, and *Newsweek* doesn't include various departments, such as Conventional Wisdom and Perspectives. This is why you should definitely take advantage of the free trial to determine if the content, as presented, will be satisfactory to you.

- ✔ **Not all periodicals are available for all devices, such as smartphones and the Kindle for PC app.** Which devices are supported is clearly identified on the subscription page. For example, if you hope to read your subscription to *National Geographic* on your iPhone, you're out of luck.

- ✔ **Unlike e-books, subscription content can be read only on one Kindle.** You can't share subscriptions among devices.

✔ **Only recent issues of e-newspapers and e-magazines and recent blog entries remain available in your library for subsequent downloads.** Older issues of e-newspapers and e-magazines and older blog entries are deleted automatically from your Kindle Touch to make room for additional content.

Older issues of e-newspapers and e-magazines appear inside a Periodicals: Back Issues grouping. Select the grouping by tapping it. The screen that comes up displays the back issues you have on your Kindle Touch. E-newspaper and e-magazine issues that are more than seven issues old are automatically deleted to free up space for new content. The word Expiring next to an e-magazine or e-newspaper issue indicates that it'll be deleted soon.

If you want to keep a copy of an issue on your Kindle Touch, follow these steps:

1. **Open the specific issue from the listing of periodicals.**

2. **Tap the top of the screen to bring up the toolbar.**

3. **Tap the Menu button and select Keep This Issue from the list. Alternatively, from the list of periodical, tap and hold the issue you wish to keep. A pop up menu appears where you select Keep This Issue.**

You can delete a saved issue by following the preceding steps and selecting Do Not Keep This Issue from the Menu in Step 3.

Expanding on the traditional: Looking for games and apps

Games, such as Mahjong, Solitaire, and Slingo, are also available for your Kindle Touch. Some people are purists and believe the Kindle Touch should be used only for reading; others like having the option of playing a game every now and then. Given that many games are offered for free or put on sale on a regular basis, go ahead and download one and see what you think. Personally, we've become quite enamored with Every Word, an anagram-type word game developed by Amazon. The touchscreen on the Kindle Touch is ideal for playing this game.

In general, games are played individually. Wireless doesn't need to be on to play a game.

Games can't be sampled — if you're interested in playing Slingo, you need to buy it. Therefore, it's a good idea to read the reviews posted at Amazon to decide whether the format and method of playing is going to be acceptable to you.

Not all the Kindle games that are for sale at Amazon work on the Kindle Touch. Make sure you see the name of your Kindle Touch in the Deliver To drop-down list (under the Buy Now button) before making a purchase.

Kindle content, including games, can be returned within seven days for a refund. You can return e-books through Manage Your Kindle at your Amazon account. To return games, however, you must contact customer service directly; you can't process a return for a game from your Kindle Touch or from your Kindle account at Amazon.

Checking Out Other Online Stores

As we mention earlier in this chapter, you don't have to purchase e-books from Amazon. E-bookstores are popping up all over the Internet, and with the popularity of the Kindle family of e-readers, most of these stores sell Kindle-compatible content. Publishers may also sell content directly from their websites. Exploring different options allows you to find some hidden gems. Similarly, if you have specific reading preferences — romance or science fiction, for example — specialized stores may have more in-depth selections and greater availability of titles in your genre of interest. The following list is not exhaustive but is a sampling of what can be found at various online booksellers:

- ✔ **General indie (independently-published) e-books:** Smashwords (www.smashwords.com)

- ✔ **Romance:** All Romance eBooks (www.allromancee books.com)

✔ **Science fiction, speculative fiction, and paranormal romance:** Baen (www.baen.com)

✔ **Professional and academic subjects:** Taylor & Francis (www.ebookstore.tandf.co.uk/html/index.asp)

✔ **Gay, lesbian, bisexual, and transgender fiction:** Rainbow eBooks (www.rainbowebooks.com/store/index.php)

✔ **Horror:** Darkside Digital (www.darkside-digital.com)

Buying from an e-bookseller

In general, purchasing from an e-bookseller is a fairly straightforward process that involves the following steps:

1. Register for an account with the seller.

   The seller usually requires your name, address, e-mail address, and information about preferred form of payment (credit card or PayPal are typical).

   Some sites e-mail your Kindle purchases directly to your Kindle Touch. If that's the case with the seller, enter the information it needs when you register.

   You can find your Kindle Touch's e-mail address in the Manage Your Kindle section of your Amazon account.

2. Add the e-bookseller to the approved list of senders who can deliver content to your Kindle Touch.

   To do this, on your computer:

   a. Log in to your account at Amazon, choose the Manage Your Kindle option, and in the column on the left side of the page, click Personal Document Settings.

      Your Kindle Approved e-mail list is in the middle of the page.

   b. Add the partial e-mail address for the e-bookseller by clicking on the lint to "Add a new approved e-mail address" at the bottom of the list.

Adding a partial e-mail address, such as @ebookseller.com, authorizes multiple senders from that account to send content to your Kindle Touch.

Make sure to add your own e-mail address(es) to your Kindle Approved e-mail list so that you can send documents to your Kindle Touch.

When you e-mail content to your Kindle Touch, Amazon charges 15 cents per megabyte with a 3G wireless connection. There is no charge for content delivery via Wi-Fi. Note this fee applies to users in the United States. 3G wireless transfers are 99 cents per megabyte outside the United States.

3. Browse and identify e-books you want to buy and then add them to your shopping cart.

4. At the time of purchase, select the format for your e-book.

   Ideally, you want to buy e-books with a PRC extension. This is the preferred format for the Kindle Touch. If PRC isn't available, look for MOBI. Other choices, not as desirable, are TXT or PDF.

Do not purchase e-books that are listed as secure Mobipocket or secure MOBI. These do not work on the Kindle Touch!

5. Complete your purchase by either having the file e-mailed to your Kindle Touch (if that's an option through the site) or downloading the file to your computer.

Files purchased outside Amazon are *not* stored in your Amazon archive. You need to back up the files on your computer. Some e-booksellers offer a digital archive of purchases you've made. Read the terms of service to see whether this is a feature that's offered. You may want to check whether there's any restriction on the number of files that can be stored and the length of time that your digital library will remain active.

Choosing a compatible file format for purchased e-books

The following formats are compatible with the Kindle Touch:

- ✔ **AZW** is the proprietary format developed by Amazon for its Kindle-compatible e-books. Content purchased from Amazon has this extension.

- ✔ **PRC** stands for *Palm Resource Compiler*. It's equivalent to MOBI and is the standard file format for the Kindle family of e-readers.

- ✔ **MOBI** is a file format developed by Mobipocket; it's widely used and compatible with the Kindle Touch. Note, however, that secure Mobipocket or secure MOBI files do *not* work on a Kindle Touch.

- ✔ **TXT** is a simple text file.

- ✔ **AA** and **AAX** are audio files.

- ✔ **MP3** is a music file.

- ✔ **PDF** is the Adobe Portable Document Format. The newest generation Kindle e-readers, including the Kindle Touch, have a built-in PDF reader. You can either e-mail the file to your Kindle Touch or copy it to the Kindle Touch via USB.

DOC is a file created by the word-processing program, Microsoft Word. A DOC can be converted to work on the Kindle Touch. The easiest method for conversion is to e-mail the file to your Kindle e-mail address. We discuss other options, such as using conversion software, in detail in Chapter 4.

Transferring files from your computer to the Kindle Touch

Although e-mailing a document to your Kindle Touch is fast and easy, connecting your Kindle via USB cable and transferring e-books via drag-and-drop is also very simple. Both Macintosh and Windows users can download and transfer Kindle content, personal documents, and MP3 and Audible files from their computers to their Kindles through the USB connection. When the Kindle is plugged into a computer, it appears as a removable mass-storage device.

To transfer files via USB cable, your computer must meet the following system requirements:

- **PC:** Windows 2000 or later.
- **Macintosh:** Mac OS X 10.2 or later.
- **USB port:** An available port or an attached USB hub with an available port.

To connect your Kindle Touch to your computer:

1. **Plug the larger end of the USB cable into an available USB port or a powered USB hub connected to the computer, and connect the other end of the USB cable to the micro-USB port on the bottom of the Kindle Touch.**

   When connected to the PC, the Kindle Touch goes into USB drive mode, and its battery is recharged by the computer. Wireless service is temporarily shut off. Also, the Kindle isn't usable as a reading device while in USB drive mode, but returns right to where you were when you eject the device from your computer.

2. **When your Kindle Touch is connected, simply drag and drop (or copy and paste) the file from your computer's hard drive to the Kindle Touch.**

   For e-books, make sure to place the file in the documents folder on the Kindle Touch. If you put the file in the root drive, it doesn't appear on the Home screen of your Kindle Touch. Similarly, audio files must go into the music folder to be available for listening.

Discovering Sources of Free Content

There are many sources of free content, including Amazon. The quickest and easiest way to find free e-books, games, and other offers that are available at Amazon is to search the Top 100 Free category. Not all the free e-books are restricted to classics; various publishers run special promotions to entice readers to try new authors — often on the eve of a new e-book release. You need to be quick, though — many times the freebie is available only for a few days before it goes back to the regular price.

Another option is to visit KindleBoards at www.kindle boards.com; members there maintain a monthly thread that lists free e-books from a variety of sites. The list is updated regularly to show when the e-book is no longer free.

When you order an e-book from Amazon, even if it is free, it appears as a purchase with a purchase price of $0. You receive a confirmation e-mail, too, so don't be surprised. Yes, you have "bought" the e-book, even if you didn't have to pay anything for it.

Read the fine print carefully. Many free offers are restricted to certain countries or territories. Make sure the price is listed as $0 before you opt to buy.

In addition to Amazon, here are a number of sites where you can find free e-books, all available to you legally:

✔ **Project Gutenberg:** One of the original free e-book sites, Project Gutenberg includes 36,000 books that have been digitized with the help of thousands of dedicated volunteers. As they say, all the e-books were originally published by *bona fide* publishers; the copyrights have since expired. You can search by author or title, or browse by category, most recently updated, or Top 100. Project Gutenberg includes e-books in languages other than English, ranging from Afrikaans to Yiddish. (www.gutenberg.org/wiki/Main_Page)

- **Internet Archive:** This site features millions of rare, out-of-print works in multiple languages and formats. It's especially useful for academic work. (www.archive.org/details/texts)

- **Open Library:** This site includes 20 million user-contributed items and over 1 million e-books in multiple editions and formats. Their goal is "One web page for every book ever published." (http://openlibrary.org)

- **FreeTechBooks.com:** This site lists free online computer science, engineering, and programming e-books, e-textbooks, and lecture notes, which are all legally and freely available over the Internet. (http://freetechbooks.com)

- **manybooks.net:** You can find classic texts here that are copyright-free, ranging from *Alice in Wonderland* by Lewis Carroll (CreateSpace) to *Zambesi Expedition* by David Livingstone (Kessinger Publishing). You can also find new fiction by emerging authors. All the texts offered on the site are free to U.S. users. Most titles are offered in a variety of formats, including AZW, which works on the Kindle Touch. (http://manybooks.net)

- **Feedbooks:** Another source of free, public domain e-books. (www.feedbooks.com/publicdomain)

The Feedbooks website includes a section with paid content. These e-books are *not* compatible with the Kindle Touch, so don't purchase one in error! Only the free public domain e-books at Feedbooks work on your Kindle Touch.

DRM and piracy

Digital Rights Management (DRM) is a method for securing digital content so that an e-book (or music file or whatever else) can only be read or used on an authorized device.

When Amazon first started selling Kindle e-books, they were encoded so that they were specific to the device. Authors who sold through their Desktop Publishing (DTP) platform were required to upload DRM-encrypted files. The DTP requirements have since been eased so that DRM is no longer required.

A discussion of the ethics of DRM is beyond the scope of this e-book. Just know that if you buy an e-book from a site other than Amazon, double-check to make sure the format is compatible with your Kindle Touch and isn't encoded in such a way that it would render the e-book unreadable.

Piracy is the other side of the DRM coin — or what DRM is trying to prevent. If a file isn't encoded, it can be shared freely with any number of other readers. *Piracy* is stealing e-books and taking money out of the pocket of the author and publisher. Please don't engage in this illegal activity.

Chapter 4

Putting Your Own Documents on Your Kindle Touch

In This Chapter

▶ Understanding Kindle-friendly file formats

▶ Transferring documents to your Kindle Touch via USB

▶ Using e-mail to convert and transfer documents to your Kindle Touch

▶ Viewing PDFs on your Kindle Touch

▶ Paying fees to transfer documents

*A*fter you've had your Kindle Touch for a while, you're sure to have downloaded e-books from the Kindle Store or from other online sources. But what if you want to read some of your own content on your Kindle Touch? Most people have a massive collection of documents from work or school, reference manuals, lists, maps, correspondence, creative writing, and other personal documents on their computers. Wouldn't it be nice to have some of that content available on your Kindle Touch as you travel or go about your daily life?

In this chapter, we explore how to put your own documents onto your Kindle Touch. We cover some handy services and tools to send compatible files to your Kindle Touch, and to convert documents so that they're readable on your device.

Finding Kindle-Friendly File Formats

Your Kindle Touch can't read every file that's on your computer. A file has to be in a Kindle-compatible format so that your Kindle Touch can display it. The following list describes the Kindle-friendly file types:

- **AZW, AZW1:** These are Kindle formats; most files you download from the Kindle Store are in these formats.

- **TXT:** These are simple text files, such as those you might create with Notepad.

- **MOBI, PRC:** These are Mobipocket files, which is a popular format for e-books. Some Mobipocket files are protected with Digital Rights Management (DRM); the Kindle family of e-readers, including the Kindle Touch, can read only unprotected Mobipocket files.

- **PDF:** Your Kindle Touch can display files in Adobe's Portable Document Format (PDF).

- **AA, AAX:** These are Audiobook formats from Audible.

- **MP3:** These are music or other sound files.

- **JPG, GIF, PNG:** Formats used for photographs or other graphics.

Your files in these formats are generally readable *natively* — that is, without needing to be converted — by your Kindle Touch. So all you have to do is transfer the files onto your Kindle Touch, as we describe in the next section.

Copying Files from Your Computer to Your Kindle Touch

If your file is in one of the Kindle-compatible formats listed in the preceding section, you can transfer it directly from your computer to your Kindle Touch via USB.

To transfer the files, follow these steps:

1. **Connect your Kindle Touch to your computer using the USB cable.**

   Your computer recognizes your Kindle Touch when it's plugged in and displays the Kindle Touch as a removable drive, as shown in Figure 4-1. If you go to My Computer (PC) or Finder (Mac), your Kindle Touch appears as a drive.

2. **Double-click the drive to open it and view the folders on your Kindle Touch.**

Your Kindle Touch displayed as a removable device

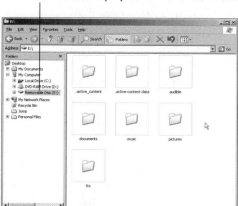

Figure 4-1: Your Kindle Touch appears as a removable hard drive when connected to your computer.

3. **Open another window and navigate to the file(s) you want to transfer to your Kindle Touch.**

4. **Drag the file(s) to the appropriate folder on your Kindle Touch.**

   For text or document files, use the documents folder on your Kindle Touch. For audible files, use the audible folder instead. And for MP3 files, use the music folder.

If your Kindle Touch doesn't have an audible or music folder, create a folder by right-clicking and choosing New➪Folder (Windows) or choose File➪New Folder (Mac), and then type **audible** or **music** for the folder name.

The names of the folders must be spelled using all lowercase. If you capitalize any letter in a folder name your Kindle Touch will not recognize the folder.

5. **Eject your Kindle Touch from your computer:**

   - *On a Windows Vista or Windows 7 PC,* choose Start➪Computer, and then right-click the Kindle drive icon and choose Eject. You can also left- or right-click the Safely Remove Hardware and Eject Media icon in the lower-right corner of the Taskbar.

   - *On a Mac,* Control-click the Kindle device icon and choose Eject.

   The files you transferred display on your Home screen and are available for you to view on your Kindle Touch.

Files that are protected with DRM are not readable by your Kindle Touch. For example, if you purchased a Mobipocket. com e-book from an online retailer and the e-book is protected with DRM, your Kindle Touch can't display it. If this is the case, you see an error message when you try to open the e-book.

E-Mailing to Transfer (and Convert) Files for Your Kindle Touch

What do you do if your file is in another file type, such as HTML or Microsoft Word? You may be in luck. Amazon provides a nifty e-mail service that converts different types of files to Kindle-compatible formats and automatically sends them to your Kindle Touch!

You can add any of the file types we discuss in the "Finding Kindle-Friendly File Formats" section, earlier in this chapter, to your Kindle Touch without using the Personal Documents Service to convert those files to a compatible type. If a document isn't one of the Kindle-friendly file formats, conversion will be necessary to read the file on the Kindle Touch.

File types that can be transferred through e-mail

The following list shows the types of files you can send to your Kindle Touch using the Personal Documents Service. Note that these files must be *unprotected* (that is, not protected by DRM) to be readable on your Kindle Touch.

- ✔ **DOC or DOCX:** Microsoft Word
- ✔ **PDF:** Adobe
- ✔ **HTML:** Web documents
- ✔ **TXT:** Text files
- ✔ **RTF:** Rich Text Format
- ✔ **PRC or MOBI:** Mobipocket
- ✔ **JPG, GIF, PNG, or BMP:** Graphics

Some of these files (PDF, TXT, PRC, MOBI, JPG, and GIF) can be read by your Kindle Touch without conversion. If you e-mail one of these file types, the e-mail service simply transfers the file as is to your Kindle Touch. You can convert PDF files to a Kindle-compatible format; we discuss this in the "Converting PDFs into Kindle-compatible AZWs" sidebar later in this chapter, along with the reasons why you might want to do this.

Utilizing special e-mail addresses

To convert your personal documents so you can read them on your Kindle Touch, send them to one of the special e-mail addresses associated with your Kindle Touch:

✔ *yourname*@free.kindle.com

✔ *yourname*@kindle.com

In both of the e-mail addresses, *yourname* is the unique name identified with your Kindle Touch. These e-mail addresses were either created automatically when you registered your Kindle Touch or set up by you if you changed them, as we discuss in Chapter 1.

To find out what your Kindle Touch's e-mail addresses are, follow these simple steps:

1. **From the Home screen, tap the Menu button.**

2. **Tap Settings and then tap Device Options.**

   The Send-to-Kindle E-Mail address displays. As shown in Figure 4-2, your Kindle Touch displays the @kindle.com e-mail address for your device. The same name is used for the @free.kindle.com e-mail address. Both e-mail addresses are provided automatically by Amazon for your use in sending personal documents to your Kindle Touch.

What's the difference between the @free.kindle.com and @kindle.com e-mail addresses? The @free.kindle.com e-mail address sends the document via Wi-Fi and avoids 3G wireless. We summarize the effect of using the different e-mail addresses:

✔ **Using the @free.kindle.com e-mail address** causes your converted documents to be sent wirelessly to your Kindle Touch, if your Kindle Touch is connected with Wi-Fi. By using Wi-Fi, your Kindle Touch avoids using the cellular 3G network for the transfer. As a result, this conversion is performed for free, as the name implies.

   If your Kindle Touch isn't connected to Wi-Fi, the converted file is also sent to the e-mail address associated with your Amazon account. You can download the converted file and then connect your Kindle Touch to your computer to transfer it to your Kindle Touch via USB.

✔ **Using the `@kindle.com` e-mail address** sends a converted file wirelessly to your Kindle Touch 3G, using 3G wireless even if you're not in a Wi-Fi zone. After you send your personal documents to the `@kindle.com` e-mail address, the converted files are sent to your Kindle Touch. If Wi-Fi is available, the converted files are sent free of charge. Otherwise, the files are transferred over 3G and a small fee is charged to your Amazon account. (See the section, "Paying Fees for Transferring Documents," later in this chapter, for more information.)

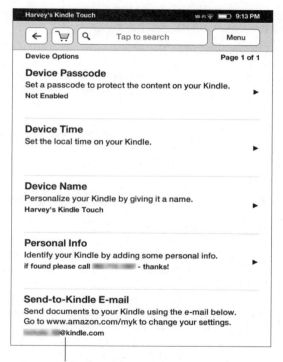

Your e-mail address is displayed here

Figure 4-2: You can find your Kindle Touch's e-mail address under Device Options on the Settings page.

More options for converting documents

If you want to read a file on your Kindle Touch that's in an unsupported file type, you can install software on your computer that can read different file types and then convert those files to Kindle-compatible formats. A few such options are

✓ **calibre:** Available for PC or Mac, calibre (www.calibre-ebook.com) can convert e-books in a host of formats, including CBZ, CBR, CBC, CHM, EPUB, FB2, HTML, LIT, LRF, MOBI, ODT, PDF, PRC, PDB, PML, RB, RTF, SNB, TCR, and TXT. calibre can convert these e-books to various formats

including the Kindle-compatible MOBI format.

✓ **Mobipocket Creator:** Available only for PCs at www.mobipocket.com, Mobipocket Creator can convert e-books from .DOC, TXT, and PDF files to Kindle-compatible MOBI format.

These tools are free and can be used to take content in a wide variety of formats and convert it into Mobipocket (MOBI) files. The converted MOBI files are compatible with your Kindle Touch and can be transferred to your Kindle via USB.

Authorizing an e-mail address to use for sending files

Amazon adds a level of security to the e-mail transfer process by limiting which e-mail addresses can be used to send documents to your @kindle.com or @free.kindle.com e-mail addresses. This prevents unauthorized users from sending documents to your Kindle Touch, and from running up document transfer charges.

You manage this approved e-mail list from the Manage Your Kindle page (www.amazon.com/myk). You're prompted to log in if you're not already signed into Amazon. Click the Personal Document Settings link in the left column. Scroll to the Approved Personal Document E-Mail List where you can add or remove approved e-mail addresses.

You can leave out the username if you want to allow documents to be sent from anyone from a particular domain. For example, adding @*mycompany*.com authorizes anyone with an e-mail address matching that domain name to send documents to your Kindle Touch. Be careful with this because you're responsible for any conversion charges for documents sent from those e-mail addresses to your Kindle Touch.

Sending the files

When you know your Kindle Touch's e-mail addresses and you've added your personal e-mail address to the Approved Personal Document E-Mail List (see the preceding section), transferring the files is simple:

1. **Open your e-mail program or your e-mail web page and log on to your account, if necessary.**

2. **Create a new message and enter the e-mail address of your Kindle Touch in the To text box.**

   You can use either the @free.kindle.com or the @kindle.com address.

3. **Attach the document you want to have transferred to your Kindle Touch.**

   There's no need to specify a subject or to provide text in the body of the message.

   You can send multiple files at once by attaching more than one file to the e-mail. You can also compress multiple files into a Zip file and then attach the Zip file to the e-mail.

4. **Click Send.**

   If you're connected in a Wi-Fi area (or through 3G if you used the @kindle.com e-mail address), you receive the converted file on your Kindle Touch in about five minutes. Very large files can take longer to convert and receive. Amazon recommends that each personal document be no larger than 50MB.

When you send personal documents to your Kindle Touch, they're stored automatically in your Kindle archive at Amazon. Up to five gigabytes of personal documents can be stored in the archive.

Reading PDF documents

Some of your personal documents that you load on your Kindle Touch may be PDF documents. The Kindle Touch can read PDF documents *natively* — in other words, without any conversion being necessary.

The Kindle Touch handles PDF documents differently from how it handles text in the the usual Kindle format:

- ✔ PDF documents display with the text and graphics laid out exactly as in the original PDF document. The layout, such as font size, typeface, line spacing, and words per line, can't be changed.

- ✔ You can zoom in on a PDF document by placing two fingers on the screen and stretching the fingers apart. Note that this is different than increasing the font size. The text does not re-flow, but instead you view an enlarged view of a section of the screen. You can then pan around the screen by sliding your finger on the display.

- ✔ You can adjust the contrast of the displayed document. The Contrast option appears when you tap the Menu button from within a PDF document.

- ✔ At the bottom of the screen, your Kindle Touch displays page numbers from the original PDF document instead of the location.

In other ways, PDF documents have the same feature as other Kindle documents. You can add bookmarks, highlights, and notes to a PDF document. Text-to-Speech is available for PDF documents. You can select text by tapping and dragging your finger across text on a PDF page. And, you can tap and hold a word to bring up a dictionary definition.

Converting PDFs into Kindle-compatible AZWs

Although PDF files can be read by your Kindle Touch without being converted, you may want to have those PDF files converted to Kindle's AZW format. The AZW format allows you to use reading features available on the Kindle Touch, such as changing the text size and margins. With the native PDF format, those features are not available; Kindle Touch displays PDF files with the same layout, page for page, as the original document.

If you want your PDF files converted to the AZW format, type **Convert** in the Subject field of the e-mail message. This tells the Personal Document Service to convert the PDF file into AZW before transferring it to your Kindle Touch.

 You can't turn the page while zoomed in on the text; you have to zoom back out first, by placing two fingers on the display and squeezing them closer together.

 Unlike other models of Kindle e-readers, the Kindle Touch does not support reading PDFs in landscape mode.

Paying Fees for Transferring Documents

As we mention in the "Utilizing special e-mail addresses" section, earlier in this chapter, you may be charged for transferring personal documents to your Kindle Touch via 3G; however, you aren't charged for documents transferred via Wi-Fi.

Obviously, only a Kindle Touch 3G can have documents transferred via 3G. If you have a Wi-Fi only Kindle Touch, your documents can be transferred only via Wi-Fi or over USB connection — so you don't have to worry about charges for transferring over 3G!

To avoid fees, use the `@free.kindle.com` e-mail address to convert files. However, if you have a Kindle Touch 3G and need the file immediately when a Wi-Fi hotspot is not available, you may decide to go ahead and pay the transfer fee. The fees charged are based on the size of the documents transferred. At the time of this writing, fees are $0.15 per megabyte for transfers performed in the United States. Outside the U.S., the fee is $0.99 per megabyte.

Wireless file transfer isn't available in all countries. For the latest availability information, go to `www.amazon.com/myk`, log in if necessary, and click the Kindle Support link. Scroll down until you see the Wireless Delivery section. Even if wireless file transfer isn't available, you can still use the Kindle e-mail conversion service and then transfer the converted files to your Kindle Touch via USB.

If you regularly convert files for your Kindle Touch, you may want to set a limit on the charges allowed for a personal document to be transferred. You can set this up on the Manage Your Kindle page (`www.amazon.com/myk`). If you try to convert a document that exceeds that charge, it's sent automatically to your `@free.kindle.com` e-mail address, for free delivery via Wi-Fi or USB. The range for specifying a limit on charges is $0 to $49.50, with a $2.50 default. Some Kindle Touch users set the limit at $0 to ensure that all personal documents are transferred via Wi-Fi and thus incur no charges.

Chapter 5

Accessories: Making Your Kindle Touch Look Sharp

Kindle Touch accessories come in hundreds of colors and varieties. A skin, screen protector, or cover is useful to protect your Kindle Touch, but these accessories can also be fashion statements. Although none of these are required, it's fun to accessorize your Kindle Touch and give it your own personal pizzazz.

In this chapter, we discuss a variety of accessories including vinyl skins, covers, and bags, plus lights, styli, plugs, adapters, and audio cables. We wrap it up with a brief discussion of damage protection policies, either from Amazon or third-party sources.

Dressing Your Kindle Touch: The First Layer

When you buy a Kindle Touch, it ships in a simple box with a USB cable and a card of instructions. That's it! Many people like to read the Kindle Touch as is, right out of the box. But if you want to dress it up, a skin serves well as the first layer.

Vinyl skins and *screen protectors* are accessories that can be put on the Kindle Touch itself. Vinyl skins are primarily decorative, although they can help hide smudges and dirt. *Screen protectors* are just that — protectors for the display that protect it from scratches. Are either essential? No, but that doesn't detract from their popularity!

Vinyl skins

One of the major complaints of the first generation Kindle was that it looked old-fashioned and bulky. Many people didn't care for the off-white case. The solution? *Vinyl skins,* which are like a second skin for all versions of the Kindle e-readers. They cover the Kindle Touch and because of their vinyl properties, adhere to the Kindle Touch without any glue or adhesive. Skin makers responded to the demand with an astonishing array of designs. Even though the Kindle Touch doesn't have the same reputation as earlier models for being unattractive, vinyl skins are still extremely popular.

The skin comes in pieces and adheres to the front and back of your Kindle Touch. On the front piece is one cutout for the Home button. On the back, the skin typically comes in three or four pieces: narrow bands for the top and bottom and a large piece for the space in between. The bottom band may be in two pieces or have cutouts for the speakers.

To apply the skin, peel the vinyl pieces from the backing sheet, place it on the Kindle Touch in the correct place, and smooth out any air bubbles. The skin can be lifted and repositioned if you put it on crooked. However, be careful if you need to lift and reposition the skin because the vinyl can stretch. If this happens, many users suggest a quick blast of warm air from a blow dryer to shrink it back to size.

Keep in mind the following hints to make skin application as effortless as possible:

- ✔ **Take your time.** Plan on 30 minutes to apply a skin (even though it'll probably take much less time).

- ✔ **Make sure your work surface is clean and well lit.**

> ✔ **Wash your hands to avoid leaving smudges or fingerprints on the skin.** Also, the oil from your skin may cause the vinyl not to adhere as well.

> ✔ **Put on the large back piece first.** Placing the large back piece first helps you get the knack of how to place the smaller pieces on the back and front.

> ✔ **Ask someone with smaller hands for help.** Although you can't change the size of your fingers, people with small, delicate hands usually have an easier time applying a skin. If that's not you, consider asking someone with smaller hands for help.

Although the skin can be removed easily for repositioning while you're applying it, after it's on for a few hours, it becomes *semi-permanent*. That is, the skin, especially the corners, stays well adhered to the Kindle Touch after it's applied and allowed to set for a few hours. If you decide to change the skin, when you work an edge free, you can pull it off easily, but it's likely to stretch out of shape. Although some users have been able to reuse a skin after an initial application, in general, plan on using it only once.

You can also reshape a skin that has been removed from a Kindle Touch using a hair dryer on the warm setting.

The following are some advantages of a vinyl skin:

> ✔ **Decoration:** For a small investment of approximately $9–$30, you can change the look of your Kindle Touch as the spirit moves you.

> ✔ **Free of dirt and finger smudges:** If the skin gets dirty, you can easily take it off and replace it. Cleaning the actual Kindle Touch case is a little trickier because you don't want cleaning solution to accidentally seep into the Home button.

A number of skin manufacturers exist, and many sell their products on Amazon. The following are three of the most popular retailers of vinyl skins with designs for the Kindle Touch:

✔ **DecalGirl:** DecalGirl was one of the first out of the gate with skins for the first generation Kindle. It used to have only a handful of designs — now it has hundreds. DecalGirl sells skins at its website and at Amazon. DecalGirl allows you to custom design a skin for a reasonable price and also gives you a choice of a matte versus a shiny finish. (www.decalgirl.com)

✔ **GelaSkins:** Another popular manufacturer with skins sold through its website and at Amazon is GelaSkins. Its niche in the skin market is that it features up-and-coming and unique artists with one-of-a-kind designs. (www.gelaskins.com/store/tablets_and_ereaders/Kindle_Touch/collection/Most_Popular)

✔ **Skinit:** This company has captured the market for sports teams and collegiate logos. Skinit is officially licensed to sell skins representing teams from the NFL, MLB, NHL, NBA, and MLS, along with an impressive number of colleges. If you want to proudly display the logo of your alma mater, Skinit is the place to go. It also offers the possibility to design your own skins, which is a nice option to display your own art or photographs — even pictures of your children. (www.skinit.com)

Skins aren't just for the Kindle family of e-readers. All the manufacturers listed here make skins for a wide variety of devices, including laptops, smartphones, and gaming consoles.

Screen protectors

Screen protectors are just what the name implies — a plastic covering for the screen to keep it safe from scratches and finger smudges. Users have mixed opinions regarding whether they're necessary. On one hand, the screen is the most delicate part of the Kindle Touch, and although you can wipe off a smudge, a scratch is permanent. A screen protector can be an inexpensive way to provide a layer of extra security for your device. On the other hand, many users complain about screen protectors: They can be difficult to apply and obscure the screen, making reading more difficult. Because the Kindle Touch is all about reading, having something that interferes with that isn't a bonus according to many users.

Keep in mind, the Kindle Touch is a touchscreen device. You do need to put your fingers on the screen to turn the pages, look up words in the dictionary, or buy e-books from the Kindle Store. The screen will get dirty. Plus, you may sneeze on it or splash milk while eating a bowl of cereal. We leave the decision of whether the screen protector is necessary up to you.

The following manufacturers offer a variety of screen protectors for sale:

✔ **BoxWave:** Offers two screen protectors, one with an anti-glare feature and a second with crystal-clear viewing. (www.boxwave.com/amazon-kindle-touch-screen-protectors/bwdcd/zpzt-g)

✔ **BodyGuardz:** Makes a combination skin/screen protector that covers the entire body of the Kindle Touch. They also make screen protectors that are available in anti-glare or classic clear. (www.body guardz.com/catalogsearch/result/index?q=kin dle&x=0&y=0&devices=1453)

✔ **M-Edge:** Sells a three-pack of screen protectors that includes a cleaning cloth. (www.medgestore. com/products/nook-screen.psp?device= kindletouch1)

When searching for screen protectors, make sure to specify your device — the Kindle Touch — or a 6-inch screen device. Screen protectors for earlier versions of the Kindle may not fit the screen of the Kindle Touch.

Protecting Your Kindle Touch with Covers, Sleeves, and Jackets

If you want only one add-on for your Kindle Touch, we suggest a cover, sleeve, or jacket because it adds a layer of protection, keeping your Kindle Touch, particularly the screen, safe from damage. (Nothing is foolproof, but having the screen covered when the Kindle Touch isn't in use is a good idea.) Here are the differences among covers, jackets, and sleeves:

- **Covers:** In general, a Kindle Touch cover is kept on the device at all times, even while reading. Most covers fold back for reading and when closed, have some sort of snap, buckle, or elastic to keep it securely shut.

- **Jackets:** A jacket is like a bag or suit for your Kindle Touch; the Kindle Touch goes inside, and the jacket is secured with a zipper. Some are see-through vinyl to provide protection while reading near water or in dusty areas.

- **Sleeves:** Neoprene sleeves are usually close fitting; they may or may not have a zipper closure. In general, users who opt not to use a cover (they prefer to read their Kindle Touch *naked*) may choose to keep their Kindle Touch in a sleeve during non-reading times for protection.

The first generation Kindle shipped with a cover, but current models do not. That gives you free rein to search for something that suits your taste and fits your budget. Covers, sleeves, and jackets are probably the most popular Kindle Touch accessories, so you have plenty of options to choose from!

Covers galore!

Kindle Touch covers are available in a wide variety of materials, from fabric to leather to neoprene, at price points ranging from less than $20 to more than $200. To get a sense of the variety out there, go to Amazon (www. amazon.com), and on the navigation menu at the left, choose Kindle⇨Accessories. Covers are featured prominently on the page.

Securing the Kindle Touch in a cover

Most covers feature one of two options to secure the Kindle Touch in place:

- ✔ **Tabs:** These covers have sewn-in tabs or elastic in each corner. Simply slip the Kindle Touch under the tab in each corner, and it's held in place. Figure 5-1 shows a Belkin cover with tabs.

- ✔ **Drop-in/snap-in:** The Kindle Touch drops into a snap-in frame that holds it securely. This design is used on the Amazon cover with a built-in light as well as covers from Pad & Quill (www.padandquill.com/cases-for-kindle-nook-ereader/case-for-kindle-touch-mini-keeper.html). Figure 5-2 illustrates the Pad & Quill cover without a Kindle, showing the drop-in/snap-in holder.

Oberon Design, a small, family-owned business based in Santa Rosa, California, makes very popular hand-tooled, leather Kindle covers. Figure 5-3 shows a variety of Kindles in three of the more popular Oberon designs: red Gingko; purple Roof of Heaven; and navy Hokusai Wave. The covers are sold only through its website and not at Amazon. Visit www.oberon design.com to find out more.

Figure 5-1: An example of a cover that uses tabs to hold the Kindle Touch in place.

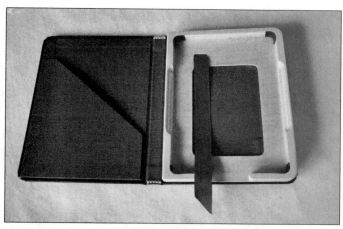

Figure 5-2: A Pad & Quill cover without a Kindle inserted in the case.

Figure 5-3: A variety of Kindles in Oberon covers.

Covers with lights

The Kindle screen isn't backlit, so you need a light for reading when you're in a dimly lit place. A popular innovation is a cover with a light that attaches or is even built-in. Amazon has a unique approach with the latter: The light draws its power from the Kindle and doesn't require a battery of its own. The single LED light turns out from the top. Figure 5-4 shows the lighted Amazon Kindle Touch cover.

Figure 5-4: An Amazon Kindle cover with a built-in light.

M-Edge makes the e-Luminator Touch Booklight, which is compatible with all of its Kindle covers. Although the light isn't built-in, it snaps on to M-Edge covers and is a very popular option with Kindle owners. You can find out more at www.medgestore.com/products/kindle3-eluminator touch.psp.

Although most covers open like a book, from right to left, Marware (www.marware.com/ecoflip-kindle-touch-cover) makes a flip cover that opens from the bottom to the top. The cover folds back and when secured with the strap, allows you to stand the Kindle Touch up, which makes hands-free reading a breeze.

Sleeves for bare-naked reading

Some people prefer to read their Kindle Touch without the encumbrance of a cover. If that's you, consider a sleeve for protection rather than a cover. Sleeves come in a wide variety of materials at many different price points.

If you're crafty, you might even consider making your own sleeve! You can buy a pattern to make a Kindle sleeve from Birdiful Stitches. You can find details to order online at `www.etsy.com/listing/55622726/padded-e-reader-sleeve-sewing-pattern.`

Sleeves are usually tight-fitting and may not have a zipper, snap, or other sort of closure device. They protect the Kindle when you aren't reading it — and that's about it. You don't have a place to attach your reading light or store your charger. On the plus side, sleeves are small and don't add a lot of extra bulk to your device. A Kindle Touch in a sleeve can easily slip into a purse, messenger bag, or briefcase.

A variation on a sleeve is the *Kindle Envelope,* made by Timbuk2; it's made of nylon with a fold-over flap secured with Velcro. The Envelope can be purchased at Amazon, and it gets very high ratings from users for its attractiveness and secure protection. Read more about it here: `www.amazon.com/Timbuk2-Kindle-ENVELOPE-SLEEVE-Gunmetal/dp/B005K2Z2O2/ref=sr_1_9?s=fiona-hardware&ie=UTF8&qid=1324217168&sr=1-9.`

Zip into a jacket!

A jacket is considered by many as the best choice for protection and convenience. Jackets are typically made of fabric, such as canvas or microfiber. The Kindle is secured inside, usually by corner tabs. Jackets have a zipper closure that provides more security than a cover. They also may have extra features, such as a pocket on the front or a place to store a reading light. Users like jackets for providing all-in-one security in a convenient, lightweight package. A wide variety of jackets are sold in the Kindle Store at Amazon. Choose Kindle Store from the Search drop-down list, enter **accessories jackets** on the search bar, and click Go.

M-Edge has a design-your-own jacket site: *MyEdge*. Kindle Touch jackets are priced at $40 and allow you to use your own artwork or photographs for the cover. To find out more and sign up for e-mail notifications about the service, visit `http://app.medgestore.com/customize`.

Protect your Kindle Touch from the elements: Plastic jackets

The Kindle Touch is a delicate electronic device that can be damaged by moisture, dust, sand, or soot. If you regularly read outside at the beach or next to the pool, consider a plastic jacket or case to protect your device. The following are two popular options:

✔ **The Medium Whanganui case from Aquapac:** This case floats if it falls overboard and is submersible up to 15 feet. The company is based in London. (`www.aquapac.net/worldstore/water-electronics-medium-875-0.html`)

✔ **Waterproof cases by TrendyDigital:** Offers a variety of options available on the WaterGuard case, including different colors and padding. (`http://trendydigital.com/index.php?main_page=index&cPath=4_41_44`)

Tip: The Kindle Touch fits nicely in a plastic one-quart reclosable storage bag. This is an inexpensive alternative to a purchased plastic jacket and is likely already in your kitchen drawer. Plus, the Kindle Touch screen is still easily readable, and the touchscreen still works for navigating and searching.

Adding a Final Layer of Protection with Bags and Cases

Many Kindle Touch owners don't consider their accessorizing complete until they add a bag or case to their Kindle Touch's wardrobe. Bags range in size from very petite — essentially a sleeve — to larger models that allow you to easily tote your Kindle, cover, charging cable, portable light, and whatever else you might have on hand. What differentiates a bag or case from a sleeve or jacket is that bags and cases usually have some sort of strap for carrying: a wristlet, a shoulder strap, or even fanny packs to attach your Kindle Touch to your belt or wear around your waist. Bags are also usually padded, adding one more layer of protection for the Kindle Touch screen.

Borsa Bella bags (www.borsabella.com/ereader-bags) are extremely popular with Kindle Touch owners. The owner, Melissa Wisen, makes bags in a wide variety fabrics and sizes. She can even personalize your bag with monogramming!

Putting On the Finishing Touches with External Accessories

So far, all the accessories that we discuss have been things to put on your Kindle Touch or put your Kindle Touch into. For the finishing touch, we talk about external accessories: reading lights, styli, chargers, and more. Once again, you have plenty of options to choose from!

Portable reading lights

The e-ink screen on the Kindle Touch isn't backlit, so an external light source is required for reading — same as with a printed book. That light could be next to your chair or over your head, or it could be attached to your Kindle Touch cover. Portable reading lights are an extremely popular accessory, particularly if you're in a situation where you don't know how adequate the lighting will be, such as a hotel room, bus, or train. With the increasing popularity of e-readers, the variety of portable reading lights has boomed in recent years. The following are some suggestions to help you select the best light for your reading needs.

Powering up your reading light: Rechargeable versus battery operated

A reading light needs a power source. In general, rechargeable lights tend to be lighter in weight (no batteries to add weight) and more expensive than lights that use batteries. Of course, with a battery-operated light, you have the battery replacement cost to factor into your ongoing expense. If you expect to use the light on a daily basis, a rechargeable model might be more cost-effective in the long run. You can use rechargeable batteries in a battery-operated light, which might save some money for purchasing batteries; however, you still have to contend with the added weight.

If you look at battery-operated lights, make sure to determine what type of battery is required. AA or AAA batteries are widely available and usually cost less than more specialized disk batteries that some lights require. On the other hand, two AA batteries can add significant weight to your light — another point to keep in mind.

 No matter what sort of battery your light uses, always keep a spare set on hand. Nothing is worse than having your light go dead at the most exciting part of your e-book!

Amazon makes a cover with a built-in light, the Kindle Touch Lighted Leather Cover (refer to Figure 5-4). The light draws its power from the Kindle Touch, through two contacts at the bottom of the cover that connect to the battery contacts on the Kindle Touch. At the present time, this is the only cover on the market with this feature.

Lights for specific covers

A few lights on the market are designed to work with specific covers, such as the e-Luminator Touch Booklight from M-Edge. This light is compatible with all the current M-Edge covers for the Kindle Touch. Note that earlier versions of the e-Luminator Booklight, designed for the second generation Kindle, are too big for the current cover designs. Be careful when shopping and make sure to check the fine print.

A stylus for the touchscreen

One new accessory option for Kindle Touch owners is a stylus for the touchscreen. Why use a stylus? Some people prefer the more precise tip to tap the screen and menu options. Others find it keeps the screen cleaner — no need to worry about dirt and oils on your fingers getting on the screen. If you're searching for a stylus for your Kindle Touch, it needs to be broad-tipped. *Capacitive styli* are a good choice as they usually meet this requirement.

BoxWave makes a small bullet-style stylus that has an attachment to hang on a keychain. They also make a combo stylus that has a ballpoint pen on one end and capacitive foam at the other. You can find out more about both these items here: www.boxwave.com/amazon-kindle-touch-stylus/bwdcd/zpzt-z. Amazon also sells a number of different styli at a variety of price points. Just search for *Kindle Touch stylus* in the Kindle Store.

Chargers and cables

The Kindle Touch needs to be charged on a periodic basis; it comes with a USB cable to do this. Unlike previous versions of the Kindle, it doesn't ship with a plug adapter. You can purchase one from Amazon for $14.99. Plug adapters from earlier versions work with the Kindle Touch. Adapters from other devices, such as the iPhone, are also compatible. Although the cable alone is sufficient, having a backup is a good idea, especially if you're prone to misplacing things. The complete unit — cable and plug — costs $25. The cable alone is $10.

If your Kindle Touch breaks and needs to be exchanged, don't send the USB cable back — in case Customer Service doesn't remember to tell you this. They want you to send only the Kindle Touch. You receive another cable with your replacement.

Amazon sells plug adapters that work in countries outside the U.S., including the United Kingdom (Type G, UK), the European Union (EU Universal), and Australia (Type I, AU). If you regularly travel to any of these countries, buying an adapter specific for that region might be a worthwhile investment.

If you spend a lot of time in your car, consider a charger that plugs into the power source/cigarette lighter in your vehicle. Gomadic makes an adapter that works with the Kindle Touch; it's sold at Amazon.

Headphones and audio cables

The Kindle can play MP3 files, and it has a headphone jack so that you can use headphones to listen to music while you read. You can also have e-books read to you via the Text-to-Speech feature, if it's enabled for the e-book.

Within an e-book, tap the upper area of the screen to bring up the toolbar and then tap the Menu button. Text-to-Speech is the last item on the menu that appears.

In the car, listening to an e-book or music with headphones can be dangerous, and in some states, it's illegal. A better option, if your car is equipped with an audio jack, is to get an audio cable to play the e-book (or music) through the car's speaker system. An example is the Kensington Car Audio Auxiliary cable, sold by Amazon. The cost is usually less than $10 (www.amazon.com/Kensington-Audio-Cable-iPhone-iPod/dp/B0031U1ATG). If you don't have an audio jack, you can get a car audio cassette adapter. These are quite inexpensive and widely available. Search for *cassette adapter* on Amazon to get an idea of what's offered. If your car doesn't have a cassette player, look into getting a FM transmitter to broadcast through the audio system.

Insuring Your Kindle Touch

Although the price of the Kindle Touch ($99 to $189 depending on which options you choose) is significantly less than the first generation Kindle, it's still an investment that you want to protect. The Kindle Touch comes with a one-year manufacturer's warranty that covers defects in materials and workmanship. Amazon sells an extended warranty that covers the device for two full years and adds protection for damage from dropping it. The warranty stays with the device even if you sell it or give it to someone else. The warranty must be purchased within 30 days of purchasing your Kindle Touch and is available only to customers in the U.S. To find out more, go to www.amazon.com/2-Year-Protection-Kindle-Touch-customers/dp/B0058WLM2U/ref=kin3w_ddp_bbe2_popT.

SquareTrade also sells two and three year warranties that cover Kindle Touches from accidents and damage. Read more about them at www.squaretrade.com/pages/ereader-landing1.

Chapter 6

Beyond Reading: Other Kindle Touch Features

*A*lthough the Kindle Touch is first and foremost a *reading device,* it does offer several features that go beyond reading. You can browse the web, listen to audiobooks, and play MP3 music tracks.

In this chapter, we look at these features — and go beyond reading with your Kindle Touch!

Accessing Experimental Features

You may have noticed the Experimental menu option, as shown in Figure 6-1. This option appears when you tap the Menu button from the Home screen on your Kindle Touch. Tap the Experimental option to see the current list of features that are available.

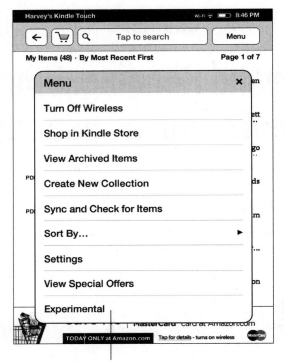

The Experimental menu option

Figure 6-1: Access Amazon's Experimental menu option by tapping Menu from the Home screen.

The listed features are *experimental prototypes* that may change over time as Amazon develops or modifies features. Experimental features, current as of this writing and shown in Figure 6-2, include

- ✔ Web Browser
- ✔ MP3 Player
- ✔ Text-to-Speech

We discuss the Text-to-Speech feature in Chapter 2. In the following sections, we offer some tips and shortcuts for using the Web Browser and MP3 Player features.

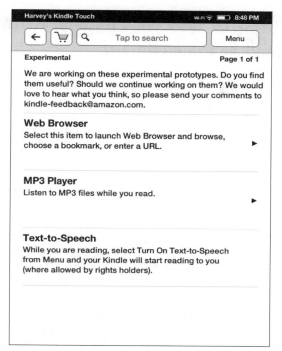

Figure 6-2: Experimental features include the Web Browser, MP3 Player, and Text-to-Speech.

Browsing the Web with Your Kindle Touch

Yes indeed, your Kindle Touch sports a built-in browser that you can use to access the Internet. The browser isn't full-featured like the one you surf with on your computer, but it is a usable, albeit stripped-down, browser that you can take advantage of when you're out somewhere with your Kindle Touch and need to get online.

If you have a Kindle Touch 3G, free web browsing in 3G mode is limited. You can only access the Amazon website (including the Kindle Store, of course!) and Wikipedia via 3G wireless. For accessing other websites, you need to use a Wi-Fi connection.

Things to love about the Kindle Touch Web Browser

Although the Kindle Touch's Web Browser is simple, it does offer some compelling features. Here are some of our favorite things about the Kindle Touch Web Browser:

✔ Even though web access is limited under 3G wireless, there are no charges for this 3G access. (Most devices other than Kindles that use 3G require an access fee or monthly charges.) You can access Amazon or Wikipedia any time, anywhere with your Kindle Touch 3G — as long as you're in an area covered by the AT&T cellular data network used by the Kindle Touch.

✔ The Web Browser provides a convenient way to connect to the web any time you're in a Wi-Fi hotspot. This could be your own home wireless network, or the Wi-Fi available in a coffee shop or airport, for example. (*Note:* Some hotspots charge a fee for Internet connectivity.)

✔ The Kindle Touch's Web Browser enables you to immediately jump to websites from links provided in e-books, blogs, or other content that you read on it.

✔ For simple, text-oriented sites, such as mobile versions of most websites, the convenience of having web access available from your Kindle Touch can be a lifesaver — or at least a timesaver.

Limitations of the Kindle Touch Web Browser

Conversely, the rudimentary nature of the Kindle Touch Web Browser has some drawbacks, including these:

✔ The Kindle Touch's grayscale display is less than ideal for most web browsing. If you're accessing sites that are rich in graphics and colors, you have a less appealing experience.

     The Web Browser doesn't support websites that use Flash or Shockwave multimedia effects.

     Java applets aren't supported. Some websites use Java applets for animations or to provide complex functionality.

     Videos are not playable through the Web Browser.

     The Web Browser is not available worldwide; it may be unavailable in some countries outside the U.S.

Getting online

As we note earlier in this chapter, the Web Browser feature is available from the Experimental menu. To access this feature:

1. **From the Home screen, tap the Menu button and select Experimental.**

    A screen of experimental features appears (refer to Figure 6-2).

2. **Tap the Web Browser option.**

    The browser opens.

The first time you launch the browser, a default list of website bookmarks displays, with the topmost being Amazon. Tap one of the bookmarks to open the bookmarked page in the browser.

Kindle Touch also gives you a fast way to get to two frequently accessed websites: Amazon's Kindle Store and Wikipedia. To do so:

1. **From the Home screen, tap in the Search field.**

2. **Type a search term using the onscreen keypad and then tap the My Items option in the search box.**

3. **Select Kindle Store or Wikipedia from the search options that appear and then tap the Go button.**

    Kindle Touch launches the Web Browser to the appropriate page with search results for the search term you entered.

You can also open the browser by tapping any web address link from content that you read on your Kindle Touch. For example, an e-book or blog that you read on your Kindle Touch may include a clickable link. Thanks to Kindle Touch's Web Browser, you can immediately access that website by tapping the link.

Browsing basics

With the Web Browser open, you can specify a web address, or *URL*. Your Kindle Touch Web Browser automatically displays the URL in its address bar for the last web page that you accessed with the Web Browser. To change that URL or enter a new one:

1. **Tap the address bar and use the onscreen keyboard to enter your desired URL in the address bar at the top of the screen, as shown in Figure 6-3.**

   When entering the URL, you can leave out the `http://` prefix, as well as the www part of the address. For example, you can type **cnn.com** rather than **http:// www.cnn.com**.

2. **Tap the Go button to bring up the website.**

   If your Kindle Touch's wireless is turned off or you're not in a wireless coverage area, an error message advises that wireless is needed.

On web pages that have more content than can fit on one displayed page, a scroll bar appears on the right side of the browser. You can drag your finger around the page to scroll up and down to view more of the page.

You can use bookmarks to save frequently used web pages and to avoid re-entering long URLs from the Kindle Touch's onscreen keyboard. Here are the essentials for working with Web Browser bookmarks:

   ✔ **Adding a bookmark:** Tap the Menu button and select Bookmark This Page.

✔ **Accessing your saved bookmarks:** From the Web Browser, tap Menu and select Bookmarks. This is also how you can access the sample bookmarks that Amazon has preloaded on your Kindle Touch.

✔ **Deleting a bookmark:** Tap the Remove button at the bottom of the bookmarks screen. A check box appears for each displayed bookmark. Tap the check box for one or more bookmarks, and then tap Remove.

✔ **Editing a bookmark:** Tap the Edit button at the bottom of the bookmarks screen. Tap a bookmark to edit its name.

Enter a URL here

Figure 6-3: Kindle Touch's Web Browser offers stripped-down but usable Web-surfing capabilities.

You may wish to zoom in on areas of a web page. Given the nature of the Kindle Touch's display size, this can be a frequent need. To zoom in on a web page, use a stretching motion on the display to zoom in. Similarly, use a pinching motion on the display to zoom out (see Chapter 1 for more on how to navigate the Kindle Touch's touchscreen). When the page is zoomed in, you can pan around the web page by swiping your finger across the display.

Special settings

You don't often have to be concerned about the default settings of your Kindle Touch's Web Browser. However, situations may arise in which tinkering with the settings can resolve problems and improve the speed of browsing from one page to another.

You can see the available options from any web page by tapping the Menu button and selecting Browser Settings. The following options are available:

- **Clear History:** Your Kindle Touch saves the URLs and content from web pages you've visited previously, to speed up load times when you visit those pages again. Use the Clear History option to delete this saved information.

- **Clear Cookies:** Some web pages save small strings of information, or *cookies,* on your Kindle Touch's hard drive. Cookies can be used, for example, to save your login information so you don't have to re-enter it on each page of a site. Use the Clear Cookies option to delete this information. You may want to do this if your Web Browser doesn't respond or responds very slowly.

- **Disable JavaScript:** Many websites use JavaScript to provide enhanced functionality, such as sub-menus that appear dynamically when a main menu option is selected. If you find the Web Browser responds slowly, try using this option to disable JavaScript.

- **Disable Images:** Depending on the speed of your Internet connection, web page graphics and pictures can be slow to load. You can choose to eliminate the images and view only the text content of web pages by selecting the Disable Images option.

Some web pages have defined areas, dubbed *articles,* that can make reading a web page easier. For example, news sites often organize their content into articles to define sections of text and graphics that belong together. You can view articles more conveniently by tapping the Menu button and selecting Article Mode. This causes your Kindle Touch's Web Browser to filter the content it displays to the desired article's text and images.

Article Mode works well with many news sites. When viewing the article, swipe the display to scroll up or down. To turn off Article Mode, tap the Menu button and select Web Mode.

Playing Music while You Read

With the Music Player feature (found under the Experimental menu), your Kindle Touch can double as a simple MP3 player. Music, spoken word, or any other type of audio content can be played through the Kindle Touch's built-in speakers. You also can plug headphones into the audio jack and listen to background music or other audio tracks while you read.

Loading music files onto your Kindle Touch

You can't buy music files from the Kindle Store at Amazon, which means they won't be sent to your Kindle Touch via Whispernet. So, how do you get music files on your Kindle Touch? You need to connect your Kindle Touch to a computer and transfer — or *sideload* — your existing audio files onto your Kindle Touch.

Sideloading describes the transfer of files directly from one device to another, as opposed to the uploading or downloading that is commonly used to describe transferring files to or from an Internet server.

Suppose you have audio files on your home computer that you want to play on your Kindle Touch. First, those files have to be in MP3 format. The MP3 format is very popular — you probably have audio files of that type already. By default, many CD rippers create MP3 files, and many online music stores — including the Amazon MP3 store — provide audio files in that format.

To transfer MP3 files from your computer to your Kindle Touch, follow these steps:

1. **Connect your Kindle Touch to your computer via the USB cable.**

   Your computer recognizes the Kindle Touch and allows you to navigate to the folders on your Kindle Touch, as shown in Figure 6-4. One such folder is the music folder.

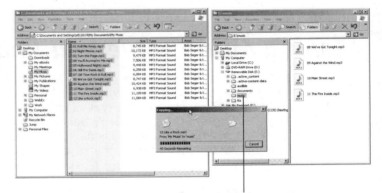

The Kindle Touch's Music folder

Figure 6-4: Add files to the music folder on your Kindle Touch by dragging and dropping files from your personal computer.

2. **Navigate to the music folder by double-clicking the Kindle Touch's drive icon and then double-clicking the music folder.**

3. **Copy and paste (or drag and drop) the MP3 files from your computer into the music folder.**

   On a Windows-based computer, the shortcuts for copy and paste are Ctrl+C and Ctrl+V, respectively. On a Mac, use ⌘+C and ⌘+V.

4. Eject the Kindle Touch from the computer. To do so:

- *In Windows 7, Vista, and Windows XP:* Either left- or right-click the Safely Remove Hardware and Eject Media icon in the lower-right corner of the taskbar and choose Eject Amazon Kindle. The screen returns to whatever was open previously.

- *In Mac OS X:* Eject by pressing ⌘+E. You can also drag the Kindle icon from the desktop to the trash can, or choose File➪Eject.

Playing music

After you copy some MP3 files into your Kindle Touch's music folder, they're ready to play! To play music from your Kindle Touch:

1. **Press the Home button to display the Home screen and then tap the Menu button.**

2. **Select Experimental, and then select MP3 Player.**

   MP3 Player controls appear at the bottom of the screen, as shown in Figure 6-5. The MP3 Player includes Play/Pause and Volume control, and double arrows for moving to the next or previous track.

The Kindle Touch doesn't have a shuffle feature, or a way to choose individual songs to play. The songs are played in the order that you add them to your Kindle Touch. If you want the songs played in a certain order, copy them to your Kindle Touch's music folder in that sequence.

A tap on the Volume Up or Volume Down button adjusts the sound level gradually. Alternatively, you can tap anywhere in the volume gauge to quickly adjust the sound to a new level.

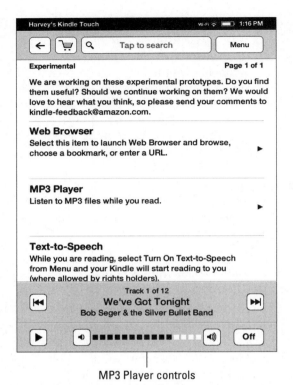

MP3 Player controls

Figure 6-5: Play music tracks using the Kindle Touch's MP3 Player.

The Kindle Touch is certainly not a full-featured music player. But the MP3 Player is a handy feature if you like to have background music play softly in the background while you read.

Music files take up a lot more space than e-books, so think twice before you load a lot of your music collection onto your Kindle Touch! You can always see how much space is available on your Kindle Touch by tapping the Menu button from the Home screen, selecting Settings, tapping Menu again, and then selecting Device Info.

Listening to Audiobooks during a Long Commute

While we're on the topic of playing audio files, did you know you can also play audiobooks on your Kindle Touch? Audiobooks can be an enjoyable way to experience an e-book with other people. They're also perfect for long commutes and road trips!

Audiobooks for the Kindle Touch are available from Audible. Because of their large size, audiobooks can't be delivered to your Kindle Touch from a 3G connection; you need to connect to a Wi-Fi hotspot for that, or download the audiobook to your computer and transfer/sideload it to your Kindle Touch via your USB cable. This sideloading works the same way as we describe earlier in this chapter in the "Loading music files onto your Kindle Touch" section, except that you copy and paste your audiobook files into the audible folder instead of the music folder. Audiobook files from Audible are in .AA or .AAX format.

Your Kindle Touch lists audiobooks from your Home screen, right alongside your other content. Audiobooks have the title and author specified, with *Audible* appearing next to the title.

When you tap an audiobook from your Home screen, your Kindle Touch lets you control the playback with the following functions:

- ✔ Pause/Play
- ✔ Forward 30 Seconds
- ✔ Beginning
- ✔ Previous Section
- ✔ Back 30 Seconds
- ✔ Next Section

In most audiobooks, a section corresponds to a chapter in the text. As you listen to the audiobook, a progress indicator shows which section you're in as well as the elapsed time of the audiobook reading.

You can also obtain audiobooks in MP3 format from online sites, such as www.podiobooks.com. You can then load MP3 files on your Kindle Touch, as we describe in the "Loading music files onto your Kindle Touch" section.

Audiobooks take up quite a bit room in your Kindle Touch's storage — even more than audio music files. Consider that before you load a lot of audiobooks onto your Kindle Touch.

Chapter 7

Troubleshooting

· ·

In This Chapter

▶ Finding help online

▶ Getting help from Amazon

▶ Troubleshooting common problems

▶ Resetting your Kindle Touch

· ·

*M*ost people find that their Kindle Touch is a reliable, problem-free device. For the infrequent occasions when glitches occur, they're usually resolved easily. In this chapter, we show you some troubleshooting tips that solve the most commonly occurring difficulties encountered by Kindle Touch owners.

For other, more complex, problems, we provide some steps you can take to solve them. And we point you to ways you can get help from online resources, from other Kindle Touch owners, and from Amazon's Kindle customer service.

Getting Help Online at User Forums and Amazon

Many Kindle owners join user forums where a wide variety of problems can be addressed by helpful forum members. Amazon has a Kindle product forum available from its Kindle page that covers Kindle Touch and all its e-reader devices. Go to www.amazon.com/gp/product/B005890G8O and scroll to the Customer Discussions area near the bottom of the page.

You can also find a number of independent Kindle user forums by searching for *Kindle user forum* on your favorite search engine. These forums usually have troubleshooting areas. Posting your Kindle Touch problem in an active forum can be an efficient way of resolving perplexing issues. Most forums have their resident experts who have seen it all and can provide quick answers to common questions.

Amazon provides a Kindle Support page with links to troubleshooting tips for a variety of potential issues. Go to the Manage Your Kindle page (`www.amazon.com/myk`) and click the Kindle Help Home link listed under Kindle Support. You're prompted to log in to Amazon if you aren't already signed in.

You can download user guides at the Kindle Support page. Amazon also offers a small selection of How-To videos, viewable from the Kindle Support page. These short videos cover common topics, such as registering your Kindle Touch, connecting to Wi-Fi, troubleshooting, setting payment methods, and transferring content over USB.

Amazon Kindle Customer Service

Kindle forums are full of appreciative reports from Kindle owners about positive experiences with Amazon's Kindle customer service. Kindle customer service representatives have a reputation for quickly resolving issues and for treating Kindle owners fairly and respectfully with their customer service issues.

If your Kindle Touch problem isn't readily resolved by basic troubleshooting steps, you may be best off contacting customer service. More than likely, a ready resolution to your issue waits on the other end of the telephone line. The direct toll-free number for Kindle customer service is 1-866-321-8851. For customers outside the U.S., call 1-206-266-0927.

From the Kindle Support page, you can choose to have a customer service representative call you. Doing this allows the representative to access your account in advance of your call, which can sometimes be helpful in speeding up the support process. You can also e-mail customer service from the Kindle Support page, or initiate a chat session. Click the Contact Us button on the Kindle Support page to initiate help from Amazon by telephone, e-mail, or chat.

Common Problems with Kindle Touch and How to Fix Them

In the following sections, we provide some of the more common problems reported by Kindle Touch owners in community forums. Many of these are quickly resolvable with the given steps.

Ghost images on the screen

Ghosting is the faint display of text or graphics on your Kindle Touch screen that may remain from a previous page even after you page forward.

This phenomenon may seem similar to the burn-in that can occur on older computer monitors — where images of screensavers, for example, can get permanently branded on the display. Fortunately, the e-ink screen doesn't burn-in, and you can safely have your Kindle Touch display a page or a screensaver for long periods of time.

If you encounter ghosting of a prior display on your Kindle Touch, you can refresh the screen by bringing up the toolbars and then clearing them. To do this while reading an e-book, tap near the top of the screen to bring up the toolbars. Then tap anywhere in the text of the e-book to remove them. The display briefly flashes black as the screen refreshes.

By default, your Kindle Touch does a page refresh of its e-ink display every half dozen or so pages. You may notice a brief flash of black on the display when this occurs. If you're experiencing ghosting issues, you can change the setting to have the display refresh with every page turn. From the Home screen, tap the Menu button and then select Settings. Tap Reading Options and set the Page Refresh option to On.

Kindle Touch freezes or is very slow

If your Kindle Touch stops behaving in its usual speedy fashion, you can typically resolve the symptoms by doing a restart or a hard reset of the device. This can address slowness or even total lock-ups in which your Kindle Touch appears to be frozen. To restart your Kindle Touch, follow these steps:

1. **Press the Home button to bring up the Home screen.**

2. **Tap the Menu button and then select Settings.**

3. **Tap Menu again and then tap Restart.**

   Your Kindle Touch displays the start-up screen with a progress bar. After a few seconds, the device restarts and displays the Home screen.

If the restart doesn't resolve the problem, try a hard reset. To do a hard reset of your Kindle Touch, follow these steps:

1. **Press and hold the power button.**

   The screen goes blank as you hold the power button.

2. **After about 20 seconds, release the power button.**

   You see the start-up screen with a silhouetted boy reading under a tree. In a few seconds, the device restarts and displays your Home screen.

Sometimes a low battery can be the cause of unexpected Kindle Touch behavior. If you're continuing to have problems, plug in your device to let it charge for at least an hour and then try a restart again.

Erratic behavior, battery charging issues, and trouble downloading content

A hard reset can also resolve other unexpected behavior from your Kindle Touch. If you're encountering any kind of erratic behavior, try a hard reset as we describe in the preceding section, "Kindle Touch freezes or is very slow." A hard reset is an easy action that you can take, and it resolves many glitches.

Kindle Touch doesn't keep track of where you are in an e-book when switching devices

Normally, you can start reading an e-book on one device, such as your Kindle Touch, and continue reading from where you left off on another device. Amazon's Whispersync feature enables you to move seamlessly from reading on your Kindle Touch to a smartphone or your computer or any other Kindle reading device.

When opening the e-book on the other device, you're typically prompted with the option to move to the furthest location read in it. In situations where this doesn't happen, the synchronization of the last page hasn't occurred as expected. Here are some things to check to resolve this:

- ✔ **Connection with Amazon's servers:** For Whispersync to work, the devices must be connected to Amazon's servers. Ensure that your Kindle Touch or other device has Wi-Fi or 3G connectivity when you're reading.

- ✔ **Synchronization settings:** If you're devices are connected to Amazon's servers and synchronization still isn't working, check your synchronization settings. Log in to Amazon and go to the Manage Your Kindle page (www. amazon.com/myk). Click the Manager Your Devices link on the left side of the page and verify that the Device Synchronization option is set to On.

If you have multiple Kindles on your account (for example, yours, your spouse's, and your children's) and you're all reading the same e-book, the Kindle synchronizes to the last page read for everyone. In this case, you may want to turn off synchronization. To turn off synchronization, set the Device Synchronization option from the Manage Your Kindle page to Off. Note that when you change this setting, it affects all devices and all content associated with your account; you can't selectively turn Device Synchronization on or off for a particular device or for a particular e-book.

Kindle Touch fails to open an e-book or stops responding when reading a particular item

If you find that your Kindle Touch freezes or starts behaving strangely when you're in a particular e-book or other content, the file may be corrupted.

First, try a restart or a hard reset, as we describe in the "Kindle Touch freezes or is very slow" section earlier in this chapter. If that doesn't resolve the problem, it's possible that the e-book file is corrupted.

Remove the item from your Kindle Touch by following these steps:

1. **From the Home screen, tap and hold the item.**

   On the pop-up menu that appears, you see one of the following options:

   - *Move to Archived Items* for items archived at Amazon

   - *Delete This Document* for non-archived personal documents

   - *Delete This Sample* for samples

   If the e-book came from a source other than Amazon, it won't be archived at Amazon. Make sure you have a backup on your computer — or have access to the e-book from where you purchased it — before removing it from your Kindle.

2. **Tap the option to move (or delete) the document.**

   In either case, the document is removed from your Kindle Touch.

3. **Reset your Kindle Touch by pressing and holding the power button for 20 seconds.**

Try reading other content and see whether the symptoms have cleared up. If so, you can try downloading the e-book again from Amazon by selecting it from the Archived Items on your Home screen.

A downloaded item doesn't appear on the Home screen

At times, an item you've downloaded wirelessly or transferred via USB to your Kindle Touch doesn't appear on your Home screen. Usually the Kindle Touch refreshes its content listing immediately when new content is added. But if that doesn't happen, try a restart, as we describe in the "Kindle Touch freezes or is very slow" section earlier in this chapter. This forces your Kindle to refresh its content listing.

If you've transferred content to your Kindle via USB, make sure it's in the right folder (directory) on your device. For example, e-books must be placed in the documents folder. If you have placed an e-book in the root directory on your Kindle Touch, it won't appear on your Home screen.

The Home screen displays items out of order

You can choose how items display on your Home screen by Most Recent First, Title, Author, or Collections. Occasionally, items don't display in the correct order.

This can be resolved by doing a quick resync:

1. **From the Home screen, tap the Menu button.**

2. **Tap Sync & Check for Items.**

   Your Home screen displays items in proper order.

Archive shows zero e-books

Your Home screen lists the number of *archived items,* that is, e-books and content in your Amazon library, as a number in parentheses next to Archived Items. You may notice (to your horror) that it says your archive has zero e-books.

This can happen if you reset your Kindle — not just turned it on/off but a complete restart, as we describe in the "Kindle Touch freezes or is very slow" section, earlier in this chapter — but you haven't turned on wireless. In this case, your Kindle has restarted but hasn't been able to access your Amazon account to re-create your archive on the device. To fix this, resync your Kindle as we describe in the preceding section, "The Home screen displays items out of order."

Kindle Touch doesn't recognize the password

You can use a password to protect access to your Kindle Touch, in the event that it's lost or stolen. If the password that you set up for your Kindle Touch isn't working, you have some troubleshooting options:

- ✓ **Be sure you enter the password correctly.**

- ✓ **Try some variations of the password.** Maybe you mistyped it (twice) when you originally set it up.

- ✓ **If you have more than one Kindle in your household, make sure you enter the password on the right device.** Sorry, we have to include this one!

Hopefully one of these troubleshooting steps helps because the next remedy, resetting your password, is rather drastic — it wipes all content from your Kindle and de-registers it from Amazon. You can recover from that, but it takes some time.

To reset your password, type **111222777** into the Password field. Your Kindle wipes clean. When that's complete, you have to register the device again with Amazon and download content again as desired from your Amazon archive. (See Chapter 1 for steps to register your Kindle and see Chapter 3 for steps to download e-books from Amazon.)

The e-book you purchased hasn't downloaded from the Kindle Store

You've purchased an e-book — or any other content — from the Kindle Store, and it hasn't appeared on your Kindle Touch. Or perhaps your subscription content doesn't load automatically. If you don't see content that should be downloaded, try these tips:

✔ **If you have a Wi-Fi only Kindle Touch, make sure it's connected to a Wi-Fi network.** If it is, the Wi-Fi indicator displays in the top-right corner of the Home screen. You need to be connected to Wi-Fi in order to download e-books and other content from the Kindle Store.

✔ **If you have a Kindle Touch 3G, ensure that it's either connected to a Wi-Fi network or is in a 3G coverage area.** The strength of the 3G signal displays with five bars at the top of the Home screen. If the 3G signal is weak, Kindle Store connectivity may be slow or disrupted.

If your Kindle Touch is adequately connected via Wi-Fi or 3G but you're still having trouble downloading content, from the Home screen, tap the Menu button and select Sync & Check for Items.

✔ **Ensure that the battery is charged sufficiently.** If the battery level is very low, connectivity may be affected. The battery charge meter displays in the top-right corner of the Home screen.

 Another reason that an e-book might not download to your Kindle is a problem or delay with Amazon's servers. Try waiting for a few hours and see whether the e-book downloads eventually.

The Last Resort

You'll probably never have to do this, but just in case, you can reset your Kindle Touch back to factory specifications. You might need to do this to address issues that aren't otherwise resolved with the troubleshooting advice in this chapter.

A factory reset is also a way to wipe your Kindle Touch clean if you ever decide to gift or sell it.

To reset your Kindle Touch to its original out-of-the-box state, follow these steps:

1. **From the Kindle Touch Home screen, tap the Menu button and select Settings.**

2. **Tap Menu again and select Reset to Factory Defaults.**

   Your Kindle Touch restarts. When it restarts, you have to register it with Amazon and download your Kindle e-books and other content from your archived sub-sections again. You also need to re-transfer any personal documents that you've loaded on your Kindle Touch from your computer.

If you have a Wi-Fi only Kindle Touch, be sure to have the Wi-Fi password for your router, as you'll need to re-transfer your content after the factory reset.

Resetting your Kindle Touch is a last-resort step. Before you carry out a factory reset, try the more common and less drastic fixes we describe in the "Common Problems with Kindle Touch and How to Fix Them" section earlier in this chapter!

Chapter 8

Ten Helpful Kindle Touch Tips

*I*n trademark *For Dummies* style, this chapter contains ten questions, tips, and tricks to make your Kindle Touch more useful to you. This chapter provides concise and easy-to-digest lists of top Kindle Touch hints for power users and casual readers.

E-Book versus Print Book

Can you get the e-book version of a previously purchased book for free or for a reduced price? Short answer: No (although e-books are usually cheaper than their print counterparts). Long answer: An e-book is not the equivalent to a printed book, so if you have a printed book and want the e-book, you're not replacing the printed book. Instead, you're buying the book in a different medium. (An equivalent situation would be buying a printed book and buying the same book as an audiobook on CD.)

Personalizing Your Kindle Touch

Make your Kindle Touch unique to you. Here are a few tips to personalize your Kindle Touch so that everyone knows it's yours:

✔ **Name your Kindle Touch.** Give your Kindle Touch a special name that reflects your — and its — personality. Perhaps you want to give your Kindle Touch a character's name from a favorite book, a name you love (or even wish you had), or a meaningful phrase. We know of a Kindle Touch named *Catalyst* because it's a *catalyst* for reading. To change the device name, tap the Menu button on the toolbar at the top of the Home screen, then tap Settings to bring up Device Options and make the change there.

✔ **Change the font and font size the Kindle Touch displays.** Although the Kindle Touch doesn't have a wide variety of fonts, you can change the font enough to make it more comfortable for your eyes. *Note:* You have to be in the e-book (or other content source) to be able to choose the font options. Tap in the top region of the screen to bring up the toolbar. Tap the Menu button, tap the Text button (the one that looks like Aa on the toolbar at the bottom of the screen), and then tap through the choices to choose from eight font sizes, typeface (regular, condensed, sans serif), line spacing, and words per line. (See Chapter 1 for details.)

Tips for Keeping Your Kindle Touch Safe

The following list provides tips for keeping your Kindle Touch safe and in working order:

✔ **Don't drop it.** We've heard of cases where a drop from just a few feet was enough to destroy the screen. Although not every drop results in a broken Kindle Touch, it can happen. Therefore, take our advice: Treat it carefully and try to prevent drops.

✔ **Keep it away from water.** The Kindle Touch and water don't mix. A spill into the tub or pool is a sure way to turn your Kindle Touch into a paperweight. If you really want to read on your Kindle Touch in watery environments, make sure to protect it. Many users report that heavy duty Ziploc bags work well. Others opt for custom waterproof covers, such as those sold by M-Edge or TrendyDigital. Even with protection, you're taking a risk of permanent damage if an accident occurs.

✔ **Keep it clean.** When using your Kindle Touch in places with dust or sand, keep it in a protective cover. The Kindle Touch is a delicate electronic device, and sand or dust can damage the internal circuitry and make your Kindle Touch unusable. If you opt to read at the beach or the Mojave, protect your Kindle Touch with a bag or a plastic cover. A can of compressed air is great for getting dust out of the corners of your Kindle Touch, too.

✔ **Don't use, store, or charge it in extreme temperatures.** By extreme, we mean below 32° F or above 95° F (0° C to 35° C). The e-ink display might become damaged. If you're waiting on a subway platform on a frigidly cold day in Chicago, keep your Kindle Touch in your briefcase, warm and protected. Better safe than sorry, even if you don't get to read for a few minutes.

✔ **Keep it in a cover, sleeve, or jacket.** Although many people prefer to hold the Kindle Touch without a cover for reading, keep it covered when not using it to protect the screen. You can find many attractive covers, sleeves, and jackets from simple to fashion-forward, from inexpensive to pricey. To keep your Kindle Touch safe, consider this an important investment.

✔ **Don't let young children or animals handle it.** Many people ask, "How old does a child need to be to use a Kindle Touch?" We think a good guideline is that if children are old enough to read chapters in books, they're probably old enough to handle a Kindle Touch with minimal supervision. Younger children, however, especially those younger than five, might not understand that the Kindle Touch is delicate and needs to be treated gently. To be on the safe side, keep your Kindle Touch out of their hands completely. Likewise, keep pets away. We've heard of dogs chewing Kindle Touches to pieces and cats walking across the screen.

✔ **Don't leave your Kindle Touch on a chair or bed.** It is very easy to sit on it, roll over on it, or put your elbow through the display.

Tips for Flying with Your Kindle Touch

The Kindle Touch is the perfect traveling companion, helping you get through hours of waiting in airports. Many people look forward to their vacation as the perfect time to catch up on overdue reading, so of course, the Kindle Touch is ideal. The following tips help make your trips smooth and trouble-free:

✔ **Use common sense for airport security and screening.** Take the Kindle Touch out of your bag or carry-on and put it, along with your cellphone and any other electronic devices, in the screening bin. The Kindle Touch needs to turned off with the wireless off. In our experience, the x-ray screening isn't harmful to the Kindle Touch; we've traveled throughout the U.S. and abroad without any problems.

✔ **Don't leave your Kindle Touch in the seat pocket of the plane.** In every sad story we've heard of a Kindle left on a plane, it was left in the seat pocket. Don't tempt fate. Keep your Kindle Touch in your purse, briefcase, backpack, or carry-on when you aren't reading it.

✔ **On a plane, the Kindle Touch must be turned off for takeoff and landing.** In the eyes of the FAA, the Kindle Touch is a portable electronic device and must be turned off (not just in Sleep mode) for takeoff and landing. To turn off, press the power button and hold for 7–15 seconds. Make sure the screen is blank (not displaying a screensaver). When the announcement is made that it's safe to use portable electronic devices, you can take out your Kindle Touch for reading.

✔ **Never turn on the 3G on the plane.** Even though you can read a Kindle Touch while flying, the 3G must always be turned off, same as with a cellphone. If the airline provides in-flight Wi-Fi, it's okay to turn on wireless from a Wi-Fi only Kindle Touch.

✔ **If you travel outside the U.S., get an adapter for the plug.** Alternatively, buy one adapter and a power strip, and plug your Kindle Touch into that. Either way, don't assume that the battery will stay charged for your entire trip, even if it's a fairly short one. You don't need a converter for travel to most countries, just an adapter for the plug. The Kindle Touch is a dual voltage device.

If you regularly travel to the same country, consider buying a plug specific to that area. Amazon sells a Type I power adapter for Australia; a European Universal power adapter; and a Type G power adapter for the United Kingdom. Each costs $15 (as of this writing). Note that this is for the plug only. The USB cable to connect the Kindle Touch and the plug is an additional $10. This cable came with your Kindle Touch, so unless you lost it, or want a spare, there is no need to buy another one. It will work with the international adapters.

Tips for Driving with Your Kindle Touch

If you travel a lot in a car, consider getting a car charger. Charging your Kindle Touch in the car means you don't need to charge it in a hotel room, which means you have less chance of leaving the power cord, plug, and even Kindle Touch behind. Gomadic makes a car charger that works with the Kindle Touch and is sold at Amazon.

Likewise, if you travel by car frequently, consider buying an audio cord or cassette adapter. Because the Kindle Touch has a Text-to-Speech feature, which is enabled in some, but not all e-books, you can attach your Kindle Touch to an audio cord (if your car has a jack), cassette adapter, or FM transmitter so that your e-book can be read to you through the car's speakers.

Tips for Vacationing with Your Kindle Touch

The following tips are helpful when you're on vacation with your Kindle Touch. (If you're flying to your destination, see the earlier section, "Tips for Flying with Your Kindle Touch," for tips on getting your Kindle Touch through airport security and handling it in-flight.)

✔ **Bring a portable e-booklight.** The Kindle Touch isn't backlit and doesn't have its own light source, so make sure to bring a portable light with you on your trip. We've discovered, the hard way, that you can't count on a hotel having a bright enough light to read by, especially outside the U.S. Plus, lighting often isn't ideal on buses, planes, and trains. Popular models of portable lights are made by M-Edge, LightWedge, OCTOVO, and Verso. A wide variety are sold on Amazon.

✔ **Load your Kindle Touch with reading content before you leave.** The Kindle Touch is international, so theoretically, Wi-Fi and 3G should work everywhere. Even so, you may have a to-be-read list that's ten pages long. Take some time before your trip to dig out those e-books from the archive or buy some longed-for e-books from your wish list. It's a real luxury to have literally dozens of e-books available at your fingertips while traveling and not worrying about buying or downloading them. For folks going on a cruise, we've heard stories that even though Wi-Fi is advertised, it can be very expensive, which in essence, amounts to a surcharge on every Kindle Touch e-book you download.

Free Sources of Great Kindle Touch Content

Kindle Touch reading is addictive, and like any addict, you'll quickly find yourself searching useful sources of content. Here are some resources to help you augment your Kindle Touch library for free:

✔ **Project Gutenberg:** One of the original free e-book sites, Project Gutenberg includes 36,000 books that have been digitized with the help of thousands of dedicated volunteers. As they say, all the e-books were originally published by *bona fide* publishers; the copyrights have since expired. You can search by author or title, or browse by category, most recently updated, or the top 100. Project Gutenberg includes e-books in languages other than English, ranging from Afrikaans to Yiddish. (www.gutenberg.org/wiki/Main_Page)

✔ **Internet Archive:** This site features millions of rare, out-of-print works in multiple languages and formats. It's especially useful for academic work. (www.archive.org/details/texts)

✔ **Open Library:** This site includes 20 million user-contributed items and over 1 million e-books in multiple editions and formats. Its goal is "One web page for every book ever published." (http://openlibrary.org)

✔ **FreeTechBooks.com:** This site lists free online computer science, engineering, and programming e-books, e-textbooks, and lecture notes, which are all legally and freely available over the Internet. (http://freetech books.com)

✔ **manybooks.net:** You can find classic texts here that are copyright-free, ranging from *Alice in Wonderland* by Lewis Carroll (CreateSpace) to *Zambesi Expedition* by David Livingstone (Kessinger Publishing). You can also find new fiction by emerging authors. All the texts offered on the site are free to U.S. users. Most titles are offered in a variety of formats, including AZW, which works on the Kindle Touch. (http://manybooks.net)

✔ **Feedbooks:** Another source of free, public domain e-books. Feedbooks also sells e-books, but be aware that these are not available in Kindle Touch format, so don't buy one by accident! (www.feedbooks.com/public domain)

✔ **LibriVox:** LibriVox has thousands of free audiobooks in MP3 format, which can be played on your Kindle Touch. (http://librivox.org)

✔ **Podiobooks:** Podiobooks provides free, serialized audiobooks that are delivered to you automatically on a schedule you determine: daily, weekly, monthly, or whatever suits your needs. (www.podiobooks.com)

Paid Sources of Kindle Touch Content

You can find a lot of free content out there, but if you're dying to read the latest bestseller, you most likely have to purchase it. The following are great sources of Kindle Touch e-books:

- ✔ **Amazon:** Of course, Amazon is likely to be your main source of Kindle Touch content. (www.amazon.com/ kindle-store-ebooks-newspapers-blogs/b/ ref=topnav_storetab_kstore?ie=UTF8&node= 133141011)

- ✔ **Smashwords:** Smashwords was founded by Mark Coker as an alternative to traditional publishers. Smashwords offers e-books that can be sampled and purchased. Not all Smashwords e-books are free, but many are very inexpensive. (www.smashwords.com)

- ✔ **Direct from publishers and e-bookstores:** You can buy Kindle Touch e-books directly from many e-book retailers, including All Romance eBooks (www.allromancee books.com), Baen (www.baen.com), Taylor & Francis (www.ebookstore.tandf.co.uk/html/index.asp), and Rainbow eBooks (www.rainbowebooks.com/ store/index.php), to name just a few.

- ✔ **Audible:** Audible is the leading source of audiobooks with more than 100,000+ titles available. (www.audible.com)

Great Gifts for a Kindle Touch Owner

You love your Kindle Touch and so does your best friend. So what do you get your friend for a gift? An Amazon gift card or Kindle Touch e-book!

You can send an electronic Amazon gift card in any amount up to $5,000 ($2,000 for physical cards). You can select a design that's specific to the Kindle or choose a design that reflects the season or occasion. Log in to your Amazon account and click Purchase a Gift Card to get started. To give a Kindle Touch e-book as a gift, search the Kindle Store for one; then select the Give as a Gift option on the purchase page and go from there. You need to know the recipient's e-mail address to complete either of these transactions.

Other great gifts for fellow Kindle Touch owners are

- An extra power cord or plug adapter
- A cover, sleeve, jacket, or skin
- A portable reading light
- Earphones
- An audio jack or cassette adapter for the car

Tips to Convert a Friend to a Kindle Touch

Most people who experience a Kindle Touch become quite enamored with it and, as a result, want to convert their friends and relatives. If you happen to be one of those people, here are some tips you can use to help a non-Kindle Touch user see the light:

- **Try the Kindle app on your computer, iPad, or smartphone.** The Kindle application is free, and there are versions that work on your computer, BlackBerry, Android, iPad, and iPhone. Reading Kindle e-books on a device with the Kindle app is a good first step to understanding the Kindle Touch experience. With the app, a user can buy e-books from Amazon and create an archive of titles. (Realize that with the app, you'll be reading on a device with an LCD screen. You need to have a Kindle Touch or other Kindle e-reader if you want the e-ink experience.) If the user gets a Kindle Touch, the e-books in the archive are available for downloading to the device. In addition, the app synchronizes between and among devices so if you read a few pages on, say, your iPhone and then switch to the Kindle Touch, it synchronizes to the last page read.

✓ **The Kindle Touch is environmentally friendly.** Printed books require paper for printing, packaging for shipping, and trucks for hauling, which are all valuable resources that cost money and are potentially harmful to the environment. E-books, which consume a few electrons and are delivered via wireless, are an ecologically wise choice for reading.

✓ **The Kindle Touch is hypoallergenic.** Many people are allergic to the ink used in printed books. Over time, printed books can become dirty or infested with dust mites, which are also potent allergens. E-books have no such irritants and are a good choice for readers with allergies.

✓ **A Kindle Touch can help decrease clutter and save space.** Face it, books take up a lot of room in your home. The Kindle Touch can store an entire library (3,000 e-books) in a device that you can hold in your hand.

✓ **A Kindle Touch library can never be destroyed in a fire or flood.** Although a Kindle Touch might break or become damaged, your Kindle Touch library, stored in your Amazon archive, will always be available. We'd never wish a disaster on anyone, but it is a fact that printed books can be destroyed by fire or water. E-books are impervious to the elements although the Kindle Touch itself isn't.

✓ **You can save money on e-book purchases with a Kindle Touch.** A Kindle Touch does require an initial investment but, in the long run, there's the potential to save money on e-book purchases. E-books are, for the most part, cheaper than their printed counterparts. In addition, there are many sources of free e-books as well as frequent free e-book promotions, allowing you to add to your Kindle Touch library in a very cost-effective manner.

✔ **A Kindle Touch can make reading easier by changing the font size.** After you discover the convenience of enlarging or reducing the font to accommodate your eyes or lighting conditions, you'll realize the inconvenience of reading very small print. Many people with vision problems have been able to regain their joy of reading by using the Kindle Touch with enlarged fonts.

✔ **You can make annotations without harming the e-book.** The Kindle Touch allows you to make notes, highlight passages, and annotate important sections, all without leaving permanent marks in the book. This is good for the e-book and good for potential other readers, who may be interested in the content but not your notes.

✔ **Improve your vocabulary by using the dictionary to look up unfamiliar words.** When you were learning to read, you might have looked up words you didn't know in the dictionary. As you got older, you might have left that habit behind. However, the Kindle Touch makes looking up unfamiliar words easy. Instead of trying to puzzle out what *usufruct* means, look it up! (By the way, *usufruct* means the right of enjoying all the advantages derivable from the use of something that belongs to another.)

✔ **Keep your reading list private.** At times, you really don't want others to know that we are reading *The Bald Duke's Secret Mistress*. Everyone has their guilty pleasures — is it really anybody else's business that you like to read bodice rippers or trashy celebrity biographies?

Index